M000023491

LOOKING FOR LINCOLN IN ILLINOIS

Danvers Township Library
117 E. Exchange Street
Danvers, IL 61732-0376
PH/FAX 309-963-4269
www.danverstownshiplibrary.com

LOOKING FOR LINCOLN IN ILLINOIS

A GUIDE TO LINCOLN'S EIGHTH JUDICIAL CIRCUIT

Guy C. Fraker

Southern Illinois University Press
Carbondale

Southern Illinois University Press
www.siupress.com

Copyright © 2017 by the Illinois Historic Preservation Agency
All rights reserved
Printed in the United States of America

20 19 18 17   4 3 2 1

The publication of this book has been made possible by the
generous support of the Looking for Lincoln Heritage
Coalition, courtesy of Sarah Watson, executive director.

Cover illustrations (clockwise from top): state outline, by Tom
Willcockson; photo of Abraham Lincoln, by Edward Barnwell,
Decatur, Illinois, May 1860, *also appears on title page* (Decatur
Public Library Local History Collection); County Line Marker
(Guy C. Fraker); Main Street, Shelbyville, Illinois (Shelby
County Historical and Genealogical Society); "witness oaks,"
Vermilion County, Illinois (Shaw and Burlingame, *Abraham
Lincoln Traveled This Way*, 2013); McLean County Courthouse
(McLean County Museum of History); *Young Lawyer*, by
Lorado Taft (Guy C. Fraker). All photos have been cropped.

Library of Congress Cataloging-in-Publication Data
Names: Fraker, Guy C., 1938– author.
Title: Looking for Lincoln in Illinois : a guide to Lincoln's Eighth
Judicial Circuit / Guy C. Fraker.
Description: Carbondale [Illinois] : Southern Illinois University
Press, 2017. | Series: Looking for Lincoln | Includes
bibliographical references and index.
Identifiers: LCCN 2017004903 | ISBN 9780809336166 (paperback)
| ISBN 9780809336173 (e-book)
Subjects: LCSH: Lincoln, Abraham, 1809–1865—Career in law. |
Law—Illinois—Downstate Illinois—History—19th century. |
Illinois. Circuit Court (8th Circuit)—History—19th century.
| Lawyers—Illinois—History—19th century. | Presidents—
United States. | BISAC: TRAVEL / United States / Midwest /
East North Central (IL, IN, MI, OH, WI). | HISTORY / United
States / 19th Century. | HISTORY / United States / State & Local
/ Midwest (IA, IL, IN, KS, MI, MN, MO, ND, NE, OH, SD,
WI). | BIOGRAPHY & AUTOBIOGRAPHY / Presidents & Heads of
State. | HISTORY / United States / Civil War Period (1850–1877).
Classification: LCC KF368.L52 F75 2017 | DDC 340.092—dc23
LC record available at https://lccn.loc.gov/2017004903

This paper meets the requirements of ANSI/NISO Z39.48-1992
(Permanence of Paper) ∞

*To my grandson, Patrick, and my wife,
Ruth Ann, both of whom patiently
accompanied me on many of my
Circuit travels*

CONTENTS

FOREWORD

Here I have lived a quarter of a century and have passed from a young to an old man.

—Abraham Lincoln, February 11, 1861

FEW AMERICANS HAVE DEMONSTRATED THE COMBINATION OF

ambition and selflessness, integrity and pragmatism, confidence and humility, and persistent pursuit of what is right that Abraham Lincoln did. Where did he get the qualities and skills it took to steer the nation and democracy through the crisis of the Civil War?

The major portion of Lincoln's training for this task took place in central Illinois. Little has been written about his life and development from the time he arrived in Illinois at age 21 until his departure for the White House over 31 years later. The frontier of central Illinois was the perfect place for this raw-boned farmhand to hone his natural talent and intellectual skills to meet the challenges that he would face as the leader of the nation.

Lincoln and central Illinois evolved on parallel courses, maturing together. The coming of the railroads some 20 years after his arrival totally altered the region. He learned to deal with change as he experienced the revolutionary transformation of society that took place there in the 1850s. He traveled extensively throughout the region, first by horse and then by train, practicing law and pursuing politics. There are numerous sites, buildings, homes, streetscapes, and landscapes that still exist in the towns he visited and the prairies he crossed. This region felt the presence and influence of Lincoln. It, in turn, influenced and molded him.

An in-depth understanding of Lincoln cannot be reached without becoming acquainted with the region and Lincoln's role in it. Illinois became a key state in the 1850s, and central Illinois was the state's most vital area. Lincoln gained the Republican nomination for president because he built the network to do so while traveling and working in central Illinois.

The Abraham Lincoln National Heritage Area was created by Congress in 2008 as part of the National Park Service. The 42-county region preserves the life and times of Lincoln in central Illinois. The nationally significant landscape is filled with numerous Lincoln sites from his prepresidential life. The Looking for Lincoln Heritage Coalition coordinates projects, programs, and events that focus on the unique stories of the area; enhances and promotes Lincoln scholarship and heritage tourism; and stimulates economic development within the region.

This volume is the third in a series of books examining Lincoln's development and rise in central Illinois. It is our intent that these publications will augment the Looking for Lincoln Heritage Coalition's efforts to

- create engaging experiences that connect places and stories throughout the Heritage Area and promote awareness of the region's history, culture, and significance;
- stimulate tourism that supports increased economic activity and investment in heritage resources; and
- raise public consciousness about the benefits of preserving the historical and cultural legacies of central Illinois.

It is our hope that you are inspired to learn more about the life, times, and legacy of Abraham Lincoln in central Illinois and the people, places, and forces in the region that shaped and elevated him to the White House.

Board of Directors
Looking for Lincoln Heritage Coalition

PREFACE

THIS SERIES IS TITLED "LOOKING FOR LINCOLN." IN A SENSE,

I found him for myself on the Eighth Judicial Circuit. Much of Lincoln remains there: counties he helped to form, one he named, a town named for him because he was the attorney who organized it, buildings and sites he visited, and families and units of government he represented. But there is more than that. Exploring the terrain he traveled, driving on some of the roads he traversed as he went from place to place plying his profession, creates an almost palpable sense of Lincoln. Each of the county seats he visited has a unique chapter full of stories of his time there, the contributions he made to the shaping of each community, and the role of those communities in raising Lincoln to the presidency.

There is a spirit of generosity and willingness to share Lincoln tales in each community, and this book could not have been written without the people who tell them. In naming some of these storytellers I risk omitting others equally deserving of thanks. First, I want to thank Tom Schwartz, then Illinois State Historian and now Director of the Hoover Presidential Library in West Branch, Iowa. Fifteen years ago, he steered me to the Lincoln Circuit Marker Association in the State Archives, starting me on a quest to better know Lincoln that continues with this book. I extend further thanks and gratitude to James Cornelius, the staff of the Archives at the Urbana (IL) Free Library, Joey Woolridge, Chuck Hand, Ron Keller, Nancy Chapin, Ann Moseley, Nathan Pierce, Barbara Stroud-Barth, Becky Dempster, Bill Kemp, Greg Koos, John Krueger, Frank Mitchell, Beth Whisman, Bob Williams, Janet Roney, Meredith Fraker, the Allerton Library in Monticello, Illinois, Sue and Don Richter, John O'Rourke, Linda Barrett, Steve Beckett, and Ron Spears. I want to give special thanks to the talented preliminary editor and indexer of this book, Julie Derden. Before I even began the book, she suggested the use of icons that make the book more user-friendly as you drive the Circuit. I am indebted to the dedicated staff of the Looking for Lincoln Heritage Coalition, Sarah Watson, Heather Wickens, and Jeanette Cowden, as well as the patient and able transcriber of my countless revisions, Judy Matens.

As was the case with my first book, I would not have been able to produce this one without the remarkable support, advice, and editing skills of Sylvia Frank Rodrigue of Southern Illinois University Press. I am also grateful for the assistance, the knowledge, and the friendships that were extended to me at the press. I can only give a blanket "thank you" to many others who aided me and contributed to this project.

I am so pleased that this volume is part of the series of guidebooks issued by Looking for Lincoln about the Heritage Area. My main goal is to share with you the landscape Lincoln saw and the evocative, winding roads he traveled. The hours I spent wandering across the Circuit—many on the same roads that Lincoln traversed—added markedly to my search for Lincoln, the Circuit lawyer. The routes he took and the towns he visited have been carefully documented. However, in order to fit the specifications of the series and to focus on Lincoln the lawyer, I have not included numerous Lincoln sites because they do not relate specifically to Lincoln's law practice. Be sure to seek out those other sites while you are visiting the towns in the Circuit—they will enhance your journey.

I encourage you to take time along the way to occasionally stop and absorb the scene. In the quiet solitude of these near-abandoned roads surrounded by the same terrain that surrounded Lincoln, there is a greater sense of his presence than at the more renowned Lincoln sites.

Guy C. Fraker

FINDING YOUR WAY

THIS BOOK INCLUDES A GENERAL OUTLINE MAP SHOWING THE

entire route around the Circuit and its location within the state of Illinois. A map at the beginning of each of the four chapters shows that section of the route covered in the chapter. Space limitations do not permit maps in sufficient detail to actually find your way.

You must refer to the written directions to drive the Circuit. The directions will help you navigate every turn throughout the trip. *They will always be in italics.* The amount of text demanded by them limits the other content of the book. The chapter titles and headings include both the county and county seat in Lincoln's time.

Icons have been used in the text to make it easier to find the entries. Most entries are designated by these icons.

ICONS AND ROUTE ABBREVIATIONS

ICONS

 County Line Marker

 Courthouse Marker

 Looking for Lincoln Wayside Exhibits

 Lincoln Point of Interest

ROUTE ABBREVIATIONS

US Federal Roads (e.g., US 136)

IL   State of Illinois Routes (e.g., IL 24)

C   County Roads (e.g., C 050 E = north-south road; C 10750 N = east-west road). *Note*: The "C" is not part of the actual road designation. It was added by the author to identify all county roads.

I   Interstate (e.g., I-55)

LOOKING FOR LINCOLN IN ILLINOIS

Map of Illinois, showing the route around the Circuit.

INTRODUCTION

LINCOLN AND THE COUNTIES OF THE
EIGHTH JUDICIAL CIRCUIT

Abraham Lincoln spent his entire adult life before ascending to the presidency in the area of the Eighth Judicial Circuit in east central Illinois. A full understanding of Lincoln the president requires an understanding of the area where he shaped his personal, professional, and political skills.

This book will guide you around this Circuit, often on the actual roads that Lincoln traveled. It takes you along to the locales where events significant to his legal career occurred. The focus is on Lincoln the lawyer and the sites in the Circuit important to him.

From the beginning of the state and throughout its history, Illinois' legislature organized contiguous counties of the state into Circuits, and the principal trial tribunal in each county was its Circuit court. The counties of each Circuit shared the same presiding Circuit judge, who was the Circuit's central figure. Each Circuit also had the same prosecutor, whose title was state's attorney. The primary focus of Lincoln's practice was the Eighth Judicial Circuit.

He was admitted to the practice of law in 1837, and the Circuit was formed two years later. Thereafter, every two years, the legislature set the Circuit court sessions of each county in consecutive order for the following two years, with sessions in both spring and fall. The judge toured from county seat to county seat, accompanied by those lawyers who traveled the Circuit. Few lawyers visited all counties. Lincoln was an exception, as he would generally travel to all counties for both sessions.

I have chosen for the book the time frame between 1847 and 1853, during which period the Circuit consisted of 14 counties. As the state's population grew, the number of counties in each Circuit changed somewhat, as noted in the appendix, which lists all the counties in the Circuit during Lincoln's entire career, 1839–60. The period between 1847 and 1853 represented the high-water mark for the Eighth Judicial Circuit. It covered approximately 10,000 square miles at that time, an area nearly twice the size of Connecticut. The 400- to 500-mile trip around the Circuit took 10 to 12 weeks, by horse, until the arrival of the railroads around 1853. It was mostly tall grass prairie, which was occasionally interrupted by large hardwood groves and clear meandering rivers and streams.

Illinois was settled from the south to the north, so central Illinois was still raw frontier when Lincoln and his family came from Indiana in 1830. The area of the Circuit grew in population and institutional maturity as Lincoln grew in personal maturity and ability. The Lincolns settled in Decatur, a tiny hamlet that was the county seat of Macon County, which would one day be part of the Eighth Judicial Circuit. After a year there, Lincoln moved to New Salem, then in Sangamon County, where he lived from 1831 to 1837. Following defeat in his first elective effort in 1832, he was elected to the legislature in 1834, 1836, 1838, and 1840. Lincoln followed a different path than most in his profession: many lawyers subsequently become politicians, but Lincoln started as a politician before becoming a lawyer. In 1837 he moved to Springfield, which was his home until he went to Washington in 1861. Springfield was Illinois' center of power and influence during his 23 years there, primarily because the state capital moved from Vandalia to Springfield in 1837. Lincoln played a major role in the legislation affecting this move. Springfield was also the county seat of Sangamon County, which became part of the Eighth Judicial Circuit. The entire Circuit was the center of his law practice, not just Springfield.

Lincoln educated himself in the law, studying basic law books instead of apprenticing in the law office of another. He devoured these texts, which he borrowed from his friend John Todd Stuart, one of the leading Whigs in the Illinois legislature, who Lincoln met at his first Vandalia session. The first judge of the Eighth Judicial Circuit was Samuel H. Treat. A native of New York, he moved to Springfield in 1834. A Democrat, he was appointed to the Circuit bench in 1839. In 1841 the position was abolished by the Illinois legislature, and each member of the Illinois Supreme Court was assigned to a Circuit. Treat was elected by that body to the Supreme Court and was assigned to the Eighth Judicial Circuit. He presided until the Illinois Constitution of 1848 created the separate position of Circuit judge. At that time David Davis was elected as Circuit judge. Treat remained on the Illinois Supreme Court until 1855 when he was appointed by Franklin Pierce to the Federal District Court for the Southern District of Illinois, located in Springfield, a position he held until his death in 1887. Lincoln appeared before Treat in more than 870 cases on the Eighth, in the Illinois Supreme Court, and in the federal courts. Lincoln and Treat became close friends over the years, and Treat served as a pallbearer in Lincoln's funeral.

David Davis of Bloomington, a delegate to the 1848 Constitutional Convention, was elected as the new Circuit judge upon the position's reinstatement. He began practicing law in Bloomington in 1836, a year after starting in Pekin. Born into wealth in Maryland and raised in Massachusetts, Davis graduated from Kenyon College and attended New Haven School of Law. He then apprenticed in Lenox, Massachusetts, where he fell in love with Sarah Walker. Having established his practice in Bloomington, in 1838 he returned to Lenox to marry Sarah and bring her to Illinois. Davis's loving letters to her from the Circuit are a telling source about life on the

Circuit. As a Whig, he served one term in the legislature several years before his election to Circuit judge. Early in the 1840s, he began purchasing land and amassed a fortune in land during his lifetime. Davis was the single most effective and important figure among Lincoln's supporters, playing a major role in Lincoln's nomination in 1860. He sat as Circuit judge from 1848 until 1862, when Lincoln appointed him to the United States Supreme Court.

Samuel H. Treat served as a judge in Illinois from 1839 to 1887.

The central theme of Lincoln's law career is that he practiced in order to make a living. His cases reflect no other agenda, and they covered the whole spectrum of subject matter. He most frequently litigated on debt cases, routine and mundane matters, which took up about half of his time. He represented both creditors and debtors alike. Real estate disputes—usually over titles—composed the second most frequent type of case he contested, and he also had a substantial inheritance practice. He handled numerous slander cases, which were more common at the time, as well as a number of divorce cases in which he represented both men and women, plaintiffs and defendants. He oversaw a smattering of negligence cases, then less common, including several malpractice matters. Lincoln also represented a number of counties and county officials—a measure of his stature around the state. His criminal work constituted only about 5 percent of his practice, and he usually defended the accused in such instances, but on occasion he acted as special prosecutor. These included 27 murder cases. In addition to all of this, he was an effective lobbyist and had a significant office practice, about which less is known due to its private nature. The breadth of his legal experience became a great source of education and familiarity with the socioeconomic forces of the day.

Lincoln was not only one of the best lawyers on the Circuit but also one of its most popular. His high character, integrity, and honesty were enhanced by his unassuming nature, renowned sense of humor, and storytelling ability. On the long rides across the prairie, he often relieved the monotony with his endless inventory of stories, jokes, and anecdotes. The lawyers stayed in inns—called taverns—during their travels, whose quality varied from poor to worse. Generally, the food was horrible. Once Lincoln ordered an additional beverage after a meal: "If this is coffee, bring me more coffee, if it is tea, bring me more tea." These conditions often caused Davis and Lincoln to take advantage of their elevated stature to find accommodations in the homes of local residents. But when overnighting in these taverns, Lincoln's storytelling would continue long into the evening. His circuit companions, and frequently the litigants themselves, were entertained by Lincoln at these informal gatherings, over which Judge David Davis presided.

Lincoln often used humor in his case presentations as well. This was possible in the courtrooms since all the court personnel and jurors were men, allowing more latitude in the nature of the humor. Lincoln was never above an off-color story. His appreciation for ribald humor is confirmed by a letter from his close friend, attorney Ward Hill Lamon, with whom he shared much humor. In August 1860 Lamon sent him a printed form, which was a long poem with blank rhyming lines. To complete a rhyme, a crude word was required by the reader.

Much of Lincoln's success as a raconteur was due to his storytelling skill, which included a deft ability to mimic, good timing, Lincoln's jovial public persona over-all, and his hardy laughter at his own jokes. A Circuit companion once said that "Lincoln would mimic dialects, a Dutchman, an Irishman, or a Negro, to maximize the success of the telling of the story."

On one occasion early in his political career, when verbally attacked at a campaign event, he responded by imitating the speech and limp of his adversary, Jesse B. Thomas. Lincoln performed in such a brutal fashion that the helpless opponent ran from the stage in tears. For years this occurrence was known as the "skinning of Thomas." The cruelty of this event prompted Lincoln to moderate his campaign style and the nature of his humor thereafter.

His humor was often self-deprecating. He told of a woman he met on horseback as they rode past each other on a narrow forest path. She stopped to tell him he was the ugliest man she had ever seen. His response was to remind her that he couldn't help it. She in turn responded, "Well, you could stay home." On another occasion he was accused of being two-faced, to which he replied "If I had two faces, do you think I would be wearing this one?"

As Lincoln rode the endless miles across the prairie, he would occasionally withdraw from the banter and conversation to read Euclid or Shakespeare, or the poetry of Robert Burns, or the Bible. He seldom, if ever, read fiction or legal texts. Sometimes he would simply detach himself from his companions to think. Much of his profound understanding of the issues of the day can be attributed to meditation and deep thought in the solitude of traversing endless miles of prairie. Driving the hidden roads today reveals that solitude. These miles also allowed Lincoln to plan and devise the strategies that led to his political ascent. They gave him the time to consider and form the ideas and concepts that would one day save the nation.

As he traveled, he not only built a substantial law practice but also carefully constructed a political network among the lawyers, clients, and other friends he made on the Circuit. It allowed him to remain politically active without appearing to do so. During some evenings he would talk politics and make speeches, especially as the slavery issue heated up in the 1850s. His law practice and politics are closely intertwined, and the network he formed between the two ultimately became a primary force in his ascent. Still, this book is focused on the sites and events of Lincoln's legal career, not his political one. As you travel the Circuit, you will observe Lincoln sites of importance that are omitted from this book, but do not consider the omissions as commentary on their significance. The routes described herein will frequently take you to these other Lincoln sites.

The story that is told here is necessarily brief. For further details and accounts of the people, places, and sites visited by Lincoln, please refer to *Lincoln's Ladder to the Presidency: The Eighth Judicial Circuit*, published by Southern Illinois University Press in 2012.

MARKERS AROUND THE CIRCUIT

Your trip around the Circuit will be enhanced by two sets of Markers. I have created two numbering systems, one for each set.

The Lincoln Circuit Marking Association (under the auspices of the Daughters of the American Revolution of Illinois and led by Lottie Jones of Danville) placed

County Line Marker on the Woodford-McLean County Line.

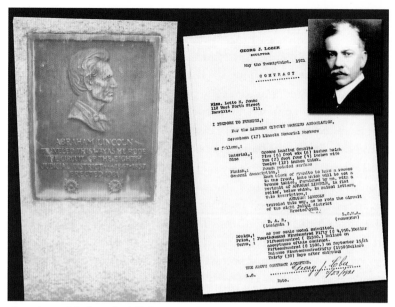

Courthouse Marker, the bill for its production, and Henry Bacon.

Wayside Exhibit at the northeast corner of Front and Main Streets in Bloomington, Illinois.

in 1921 and 1922 unique concrete Markers with bronze plaques on each county line where Lincoln crossed, either on the original roads, if still there, or on nearby roads that replaced them. These Markers serve as guideposts for the trip and are referred to as "County Line Markers." Their locations are charmingly obscure in most instances, so GPS coordinates are provided. This first set of Markers also includes blocks of New Hampshire granite placed at the site of each Circuit Courthouse where Lincoln practiced. These were designed by Henry Bacon, the architect of the Lincoln Memorial in Washington, D.C., and are referred to as "Courthouse Markers."

The Looking for Lincoln "Wayside Exhibits" compose the second set of Markers and were placed in celebration of the bicentennial of Lincoln's birth in 2009. Throughout the Abraham Lincoln

National Heritage Area, which consists of 42 downstate Illinois counties, including all those that are part of the journey laid out here, you'll encounter 262 of these Markers. You'll find 55 of these along the Circuit route, and I've summarized them in the text. They are numbered according to the order you will reach them as you follow the routes outlined in the book. These illustrated storyboards, written by Lincoln scholars, tell the story of Lincoln at a particular site. The text and pictures featured on the exhibits supplement the content of this book. Only those related to the law practice are listed and numbered. As you travel the Circuit, you will encounter many others on various subjects, and you are encouraged to read these as well.

ROADS OF THE CIRCUIT AND PRIVACY

A few words about the routes selected are necessary. The government survey of central Illinois in the nineteenth century led to many of the roads later becoming east-west or north-south, often replacing the original "most direct roads." The original roads often followed the terrain or took the shortest route. However, many of these still exist. You will learn to recognize the difference by the very nature of the roads themselves.

I have not selected the fastest routes between Circuit towns, but the most authentic. There are occasional alternatives. If you have limited time, you may want to devise a more direct route of your own.

The designated roads include federal, state, and county roads, as well as interstates. In the directions they are listed as "US," "IL," "C" and "I," respectively.

A final note: Some of the locations are on private property. Their inclusion in the guide is necessary to paint the entire picture of Lincoln's time on the Circuit, but that does not imply any permission to trespass. You should always respect the privacy of those owners fortunate enough to own a part of the Lincoln Circuit.

1. HEADING NORTH

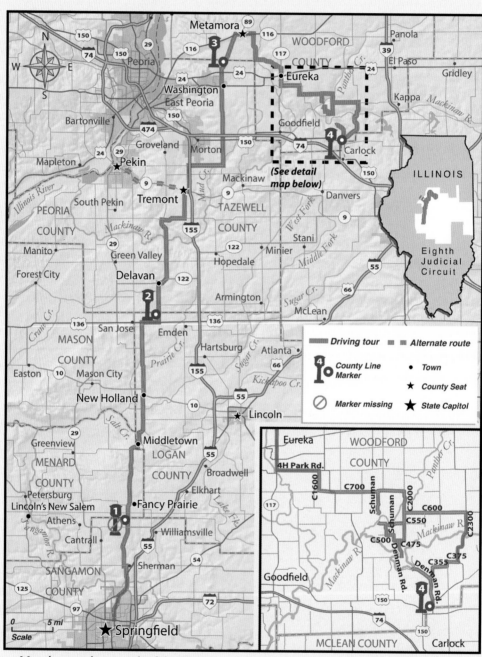

Map showing the west side of the Circuit.

SANGAMON (SPRINGFIELD)

SANGAMON COUNTY WAS THE FIRST COUNTY IN THE EIGHTH

Judicial Circuit where European immigrants, who arrived in 1817, settled. The current city of Springfield began in 1822 as a small settlement along Edward's Trace, an overland trail and the state's most important highway (today's I-55), that ran from present-day East St. Louis to Springfield. Elijah Iles, an entrepreneurial merchant and eventually a client of Lincoln's, organized the village, which was originally known as Calhoun. The county was formally created in 1821, and four years later the renamed city of Springfield became the county seat.

Until 1849 Springfield was home to the state's only federal court. Half of Lincoln's cases over his career were in the Circuit court of Sangamon County. The Supreme Court, also located in Springfield, attracted business for Lincoln from all over the state. There he made significant contacts during the biennial legislative sessions that drew political leaders from the entire state.

WALKING TOUR OF DOWNTOWN'S LINCOLN LEGAL SITES

First, the Courthouses

Park at the Lincoln Home and walk north along 7th Street to Capitol Avenue. Cross Capitol, then 7th, and proceed west to 6th Street. Then walk north on 6th to the southeast corner of 6th and Washington.

This corner was the location of the Sangamon County Courthouse, built in 1846, in which Lincoln tried more cases than any other.

Proceed across 6th and walk along it to the south entrance of the Old State Capitol.

Note the panel of plaques in a display structure on the south side of the Old State Capitol grounds. The plaque in the middle of the top row is from the Sangamon County Courthouse Marker, one of the series placed at all of the Eighth Circuit courthouse sites. When the Old State Capitol building was renovated, this plaque was removed from its granite block and placed in this wall. You are encouraged to tour the Old State Capitol.

Next, a Tour of the Lincoln Law Offices

Lincoln had offices at four locations with three different partners. They were all on or near the square and are listed here in chronological order.

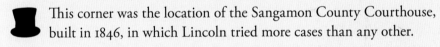

This is an east view of the State Capitol building, the construction of which commenced in March 1837 and was completed enough for occupancy by July 1840. It housed the legislative halls and various state offices as well as the Supreme Court, in which Lincoln argued over 400 cases. Note the Sangamon County Courthouse behind and to the left of the Capitol, and the American House Hotel behind and to the right.

Walk west and cross 5th Street, then north across Washington Street to the middle of the block, 109 N. 5th Street.

 First Office: John Todd Stuart, April 1837 to April 1841

John Todd Stuart, Lincoln's first partner.

Stuart was a native of Kentucky and one of the leading lawyers in Springfield and on the Circuit. Lincoln's close relationship with him was a valuable asset, as Stuart had a broad range of acquaintances and clients.

Wayside Exhibit 1: "Stuart and Lincoln's Law Office"
Lincoln's first law office was here in Hoffman's Row, then six newly constructed brick buildings, on the second floor of the fifth one. It was connected by a trap door to the courtroom, which was rented by the county, beneath it.

Second Office: Stephen T. Logan, April 1841 to January 1844

This office was on the east side of 5th, across from Wayside Exhibit 1, where the PNC Bank now stands. Its location is not marked.

Many considered Logan to be the best lawyer on the Circuit. Their partnership dominated the Sangamon County courts. A Kentucky native, Logan was nine years older than Lincoln and 17 years his senior in the profession, Logan was an excellent mentor for Lincoln, and he remained a staunch political supporter throughout Lincoln's life.

Stephen T. Logan, Lincoln's second partner.

Walk east on Washington to 6th, then south on 6th to Lincoln's third office, located in the Tinsley Building.

Third Office: Stephen T. Logan, January 1844 to December 1844; William H. Herndon, March 1845 to the late 1840s

The restored office of Lincoln and his successive partners, Logan and Herndon, is located on the third floor. The US District Courtroom was located on the second floor and could be reached by a trap door between the two offices, similar to the arrangement in his first office. Recent archeological studies have raised questions about the office's actual location within the building, including the probability that the

William Herndon, Lincoln's third partner, particularly renowned for his biography of Lincoln, published in 1889 after Lincoln's death.

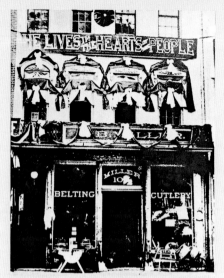

This picture of the building in which the fourth office was located was taken after the assassination of James Garfield in 1881.

BUSINESS CARDS.

A. McWILLIAMS,
ATTORNEY AT LAW—SPRINGFIELD, Ill.—Office over Freeman's store, northwest corner of the square.   feb12-ltf

N. E. PRIMM,
ATTORNEY AND COUNSELLOR AT LAW.—Will attend promptly to all business intrusted to him, both in the Federal, State and Circuit Courts of this District. Office in Telegraph Buildings, Springfield, Ills.
decl

JAMES C. CONKLING,
ATTORNEY AND COUNSELLOR AT LAW.—Office opposite J. Bunn's Store, Springfield, Ill.
aug6-dtf

WILLIAM J. CONKLING,
ATTORNEY AND COUNSELLOR AT LAW.—Office No. 4, north side public square, Springfield, Ill.   jan1-dtf

THOMAS MOFFETT,
ATTORNEY AND COUNSELLOR AT LAW, Springfield, Ill.—Office in the County Judge's room, at the Court House. He will attend to Land and other Agencies, paying taxes, collecting debts, procuring pensions, writing wills, deeds, mortgages, powers of attorney, leases, &c.
aug22

JAMES H. MATHENY,
ATTORNEY AND COUNSELLOR AT LAW.—Office in the Circuit Clerk's office, in the Court House, Springfield, Ill.   aug5

LINCOLN & HERNDON,
ATTORNEYS AND COUNSELLORS AT LAW—will practice in the Courts of Law and Chancery in this State,—Springfield, Ill.   aug5

N. M. BROADWELL,
ATTORNEY AND COUNSELLOR AT LAW.—Office north side of the square, over Ayers & Wardall's store.   jan4

STUART & EDWARDS,
ATTORNEYS AND COUNSELLORS AT LAW, a few doors west of Hawley & Patton's store, Springfield, Ill.   aug5-dtf

LEWIS & ADAMS,
ATTORNEYS AND COUNSELLORS AT LAW.—Office in the Enterprise Buildings, over the City Council rooms, Springfield, Ill.   ap23

JOSIAH FRANCIS,
JUSTICE OF THE PEACE.—OFFICE IN Court House, with County Assessor, where he can be found and will attend to all business connected with his office.   july17

HOMÆOPATHIC PRACTICE.
R. E. W. ADAMS, M. D., RESPECTFUL-ly announces to his old patrons and the public generally, that his residence and office may be found on Jefferson street, opposite Everybody's Mill, where prompt attention

Tinsley Building included the structure immediately to the south. When Lincoln's partnership with Logan dissolved at the end of 1844, Lincoln stayed in the building and was joined by Herndon in March 1845. Here they had an office until the late 1840s, when they moved to another location.

Walk east to cross 5th, then north to the office of the state treasurer. A Wayside Exhibit is on the south side of the door.

Wayside Exhibit 2: "Office of Lincoln and Herndon"

Fourth Office: William H. Herndon, late 1840s to April 15, 1865

Lincoln and Herndon's second office was located on the second floor in the back of the second building south of the Washington Street corner. This was their office from the late 1850s for the rest of Lincoln's life. It was to this office that Lincoln came on his last day in Springfield on February 10, 1861, to bid "Billy" good-bye as he prepared to assume the presidency. Referring to the firm's shingle, Lincoln said, "Let it hang there undisturbed," thus assuring "Billy" of their continuing relationship.

Lawyer advertisements from the Daily Illinois State Journal *on June 19, 1857.*

🏃 Wayside Exhibit 3: "Lincoln's Last Law Office"

The fourth law office once stood here, and the exhibit also describes the ill will between Herndon and Mary Todd Lincoln, who never approved of Herndon as a partner for her husband.

Return to your car at the Lincoln Home and begin your trip around the Circuit.

*Leave Springfield as perhaps Lincoln did. Start at the parking lot of Lincoln's home on 7th and drive south to Edwards Street, then turn **left** (east) on Edwards. Turn **left** (north) on 9th Street. Note that when the street curves slightly to the northeast, it becomes Peoria Road. Take Peoria across Sangamon Avenue and proceed north past the Illinois State Fairgrounds to N. Peoria Road (Alt I-55). Turn **right** (east) and cross the Sangamon River. As you proceed, you will see that Peoria Road is variously labeled as Peoria Road or Peoria Street.*

🎩 The Sangamon River is a thread that runs through Lincoln's entire time in Illinois. His first home in Illinois was southwest of Decatur on the Sangamon, as was his second home in New Salem. Lincoln crossed the river countless times as he traveled for law and politics during the next 23 years. The route around the Circuit crosses it four times.

*Proceed north from the Sangamon to the traffic light at Old Tipton School Road. Turn **left** and proceed west, then north on Old Tipton School Road to the T intersection at IL 124. Turn **left** and proceed west 0.2 miles, then north 4.8 miles to the end of IL 124. Continue north across IL 123 and proceed one mile to the Sangamon/Menard County Line at the intersection of Logan County Line Road and Tilson School Avenue.*

1 Sangamon-Menard: This concrete block, located at the southwest corner of the intersection, is all that remains of the County Line Marker (GPS: N 39°58'52.1", W 89°36'99.7").

MENARD (PETERSBURG)

IN 1839 LINCOLN INTRODUCED A BILL IN THE LEGISLATURE

that created three new counties: Logan, Menard, and Dane (now Christian County). Much of the territory to form these new counties came from Sangamon, including this portion of Menard and Logan. Menard, whose county seat has been Petersburg since its creation, was in the Circuit from 1839 until 1847, before the period covered by this book. The northbound road you are now on is still the Old Peoria Road between Springfield and Peoria, named both Peoria Road and Peoria Street depending on your location.

*Continue north on Peoria Street 1.7 miles around a curve to the east. At the end of the curve, turn **left**; you are still on Peoria (C 2050 E). [A reminder: The "C" is not part of the road's official designation. It means "County" (see p. xiii).] Proceed north to the T intersection at Peoria and the Middletown Blacktop. You are now entering Logan County as you go east.*

LOGAN: PART 1 (POSTVILLE, MT. PULASKI, AND LINCOLN)

THE FULL STORY OF LOGAN COUNTY APPEARS IN CHAPTER 2.

*Turn **right** and go east 0.9 miles to South Madison Street, then turn **left** (north) and enter Middletown, proceeding to the town square.*

TOWN OF MIDDLETOWN

Middletown, the oldest town in Logan County, was founded in 1832. It was part of Sangamon County until Logan was formed in 1839. There are two historic buildings on the "town square."

Wayside Exhibit 4: "Middletown's Lincoln"

The Dunlap House stands on the east side of the square. The inn operated from 1837 to 1875 and was occasionally visited by Lincoln as he rode between Springfield and Tremont. The original building was located in the town square. Local residents have restored it, retaining its authentic feel and rustic character. The exhibit includes an excellent summary of the town's Lincoln history.

Colby Knapp's store stands on the northwest corner of the square. He and Lincoln were friends and allies in the Illinois legislature. Knapp introduced Lincoln's bill to form Logan County. A historical Marker on the north side of the square commemorates Daniel Webster's visit to Middletown in 1837. Webster was perhaps his generation's leading Whig. He had no relationship with the then-obscure Lincoln.

*To leave Middletown from the north side of the square, drive east on 6th
street to Vin Fizz Skyway, a 1911 road. Turn **left** (north) and proceed approximately two miles to the bridge across Salt Creek (C 050 E).*

In 1834, Lincoln introduced a bill, the passage of which permitted the
construction of a toll bridge downstream from the current bridge, where there
had once been a ford. Upon completion, Musick's Bridge was named for its
builder and owner. Later, Lincoln also sponsored two bills specifying the
location of the road that crossed the bridge. This stretch of road south from
Musick's Crossing was surveyed by Lincoln while he served as an assistant
county surveyor.

*Proceed north through New Holland (which did not exist in Lincoln's time),
then turn **left** on IL 10 and follow it north through town until it heads west,
at which point the Circuit road (Logan County Road 14, also C 1000 E)
proceeds north to US 136, a T intersection. Turn **right** (east) and proceed
two miles to the Delavan Road (C 2000 E). Turn **left** (north) and proceed
one mile.*

2 Logan-Tazewell: This Marker is at the southwest corner of the intersection
of C 2000 E and C 0000 N (GPS: N 40°19'15.4", W 89°32'50.1").

TAZEWELL (TREMONT AND PEKIN)

TAZEWELL COUNTY, FIRST SETTLED IN 1823, WAS FORMALLY

organized four years later. Originally one of the largest counties in the state, it
was reduced by 75 percent as other counties were formed from within its original boundaries. It provided Lincoln with a solid political base in the 1840s,
although that support weakened with the rise of the slavery issue in the 1850s.
It was the Circuit's third largest county in population during this period, and
Lincoln had more business there than in any county other than Sangamon
and Menard. Tazewell lawyers were some of the best on the Circuit, and they
included among their ranks Benjamin Prettyman and William Kellogg of
Pekin, Benjamin James and Edward Jones of Tremont, and Norman Purple
and Henry Grove of Peoria.

Proceed north into Delavan.

TOWN OF DELAVAN

Traveling between Springfield and the county seat of Tazewell was one of the longest treks of the entire Circuit. Lincoln usually stopped overnight along the way, at Middletown or Delavan.

Edward Delavan founded the town around 1840 as a real estate venture (he had also created a town bearing his name in Wisconsin). The town plat included a hotel block in a public square. Today you can take a self-guided tour called the "Lincoln Mile" that includes signage at ten sites associated with Lincoln. Only one of these relates to the Circuit tour.

*After entering town, proceed north on Locust Street to Fourth Street. Turn **right** and drive east on Fourth to S. Elm Street. Turn **left** on Elm and proceed one block to Third Street. Turn **left** (west) and proceed to the historic railroad bridge. The Delavan House was located at Lincoln Post 7 at the southeast corner of the intersection of the street and the railroad tracks.*

The Delavan House, as it was known in Lincoln's time, was built in 1837 and enlarged over the next few years. Ira B. Hall leased it in 1841, and he in turn transferred it to James Phillips in 1845. It was a stop on the

Delavan House, originally named the Colony House and later the Phillips House.

Lincoln's registration as a guest at the Delavan House on September 12, 1843, which remains in Hall's family.

stage line that went north and south through town, before the construction of the railroad. Lincoln and his Circuit colleagues, including David Davis, Stephen A. Douglas, Stephen Logan, and John Todd Stuart, stayed at the inn. Hall was a client of Lincoln's on several cases, including a replevin suit where Lincoln legally seized the horses of Frink and Company, the stage line, in payment of an unpaid balance Frink owed Hall for feeding his horses.

> *Cross the bridge and turn **left** on Pine Street. Go south to Fourth Street and then **left** (east) across the tracks on Fourth. Continue on Fourth Street out of town to Springfield Road (C 21000 E). Turn **left** and proceed north, descending to the picturesque crossing of the Mackinaw River, and ascend the hill through Dillon.*

 Lincoln crossed the Mackinaw twice on each trip around the Circuit.

The road proceeds north and rises out of the Mackinaw Valley to the town of Dillon, which had been settled before Delavan. John Todd Stuart recalled that sometime "between the years 1848 and 1850," while proceeding south, down this hill, on his return to Springfield with Lincoln, he and Lincoln agreed to disagree on the issue of slavery. Stuart, sympathetic toward slavery, became a Democrat. He and Lincoln remained friends nevertheless.

> *Continue into Dillon where you turn **right** (east) on Townline Road (C 10750 N) and proceed 2.5 miles east to Locust Road (C 23000 E), then turn **left** (north) and proceed into Tremont. (You can take an interesting side trip by turning south at this intersection and proceeding down a steep grade to another possible river crossing at an abandoned trestle bridge). The gravel river bottom here at this bridge confirms this site as an alternative crossing to get to Tremont.*

TOWN OF TREMONT

Occasionally towns bitterly opposed each other when the placement of a county seat was at stake, such was its importance to a town's success. Tazewell County's first seat was Mackinaw until McLean County was formed in 1830. Tazewell lost a portion of its territory on its east side, and the county seat moved to Pekin, a commercial center on the Illinois River. Serious diseases, such as cholera, plagued the river town. For that reason, in 1836 the county seat moved to Tremont, a town founded two years earlier by John Harris of Bedford, New York. Harris donated 20 acres to the county, and the citizens of Tremont gave the county another $2,000 to ensure placement of the county seat there. However, in 1851, a controversial referendum named Pekin the county seat, which it has been ever since. All three Tazewell seats are on IL 9, a historic east-west road that Lincoln occasionally traveled between Pekin and Bloomington. Lincoln frequently visited Tremont when it was the county seat, and his extensive practice there included defense of a case brought against his clients for maintaining an offensive nuisance in the town—a lard factory. The case was tried, and Lincoln's clients were found guilty, each having to pay a fine of $10.

Tremont is home to three historic sites: the former county courthouse location, John Harris's House, and John Jones's House.

To reach the first site, turn **right** *(east) on Franklin Street and then make an immediate* **left***, still on Locust, and drive one block to Washington Street. Turn* **right** *on Washington and proceed to the southwest corner of the intersection of Washington and Broadway.*

A historical Marker describes the square on which the courthouse was located. The area includes the Franklin House, a tavern where Lincoln stayed. In 1839 Lincoln left his coat at the Franklin House and wrote a letter to

The Tazewell County Courthouse in Tremont was constructed in 1836 by William F. Flagg.

the proprietor requesting that he wrap the coat in a heavy cloth and return it to Springfield by stagecoach.

*Proceed east on Washington Street to S. Chestnut Street. Go **right** (south) on Chestnut, one block to Franklin, and turn **left** (east). On the south side of the street is the home of John Harris (405 Franklin).*

In 1845 John Harris constructed this house that Lincoln frequently visited. Lincoln rendered a written opinion to Harris that the land Harris gifted to the county would revert to him if the county seat was moved. When the move happened, Lincoln brought suit for Harris to recover the land. Judge Davis ruled against Harris and the Illinois Supreme Court affirmed that the condition of reverter was not written in the deed, so it was unenforceable.

*Turn around and return to Chestnut. Turn **right** on Chestnut and proceed north to E. South Street. Turn **right** (east) on South and proceed one block to the house known as the Red Brick on the south side of the street.*

This red brick house where Lincoln frequently stayed was the home of attorney John Jones, Circuit clerk from 1837 to 1857. In April 1851 Jones hosted a dinner in the yard west of the house to commemorate the last session of the court in Tremont before the county seat moved to Pekin. Lincoln and Judge Davis were among the many notables present.

*Turn **left** on the next intersecting street and go north to IL 9. Then turn **left** (west) on IL 9 and proceed approximately seven miles into Pekin.*

TOWN OF PEKIN

Before the railroads arrived, Pekin served as the port on the Illinois River for the west side of the Circuit. The original city of Pekin, known as "Town Site," sits on top of a gentle hill that descends to the edge of the river, providing a natural levee. One of David Davis's favorite places to spend the night was Mrs. Wilson's boardinghouse on the west side of the square; the exact location is undetermined.

*You are entering Pekin on Court Street. Proceed on Court to 8th Street. Turn **right** on Eighth and then take the next **left** on Broadway. Continue on Broadway through the next intersection (IL 9) and immediately take the*

This courthouse was built in 1848 in anticipation of the county seat move.

*angle **right**, which places you again on Court Street. Proceed into downtown and then to the courthouse.*

 On one occasion in the Pekin courtroom, a trapped bat flew wildly around the chamber. The judge enlisted the lanky Lincoln to drive it out. At first he tried to do so by twirling his coat after the bat, but when that failed to work, he got a broom and successfully drove the flying rodent out the window.

Note the Courthouse Marker on the north side of the courthouse.

Proceed west on Court to Main Street (then known as Front Street) and park your car.

*The next stop on the Circuit was Metamora, the county seat of Woodford County. Return east on Court, which merges into Broadway. Drive out of town east on Broadway, which becomes Broadway Road. Cross I-155 and continue east another 3.8 miles to the stop sign at Washington Road (C 28000 E). Turn **left** (north) on Washington Road and proceed to the square in Washington.*

TOWN OF WASHINGTON

Before he reached Metamora, Lincoln passed through Washington. The town was settled in 1825 by William Holland and first called Holland's Grove, but the name changed to Washington in 1838.

Pekin's principal hotel during the Lincoln years was the Tazewell House, sitting atop the hill at the northwest corner of Main and Front Streets, and part of the original Town Site. This site is now part of Riverfront Park, where you can sit and watch the river.

Leave the square on N. Main Street and proceed north to US 24; drive across US 24 and then 1.5 miles to the county line.

When the road angles northeast, you are driving the actual road that Lincoln took, which appears on the 1844 Peck and Messenger Map, one of the earliest maps of the state.

Tazewell-Woodford: The Marker is at the northeast corner of the intersection (GPS: N 41°44'54.8", W 89°23'48.3").

Continue to IL 116 into Metamora.

WOODFORD (METAMORA)

WOODFORD COUNTY WAS FORMED IN 1841, CARVED OUT OF

Tazewell and McLean Counties. One of the smallest counties in the Circuit, its court sessions typically lasted just two to three days. Its first county seat was Versailles, which moved to Metamora after two years. Eureka, known in Lincoln's time as Walnut Grove, became the third in 1896.

TOWN OF METAMORA

Metamora was originally called Hanover. When it was discovered that Illinois already had a town of that name, it was changed to Metamora. The name was selected by the wife of Peter Willard, a prominent merchant and supporter of Lincoln. The source of the name is a popular play of 1829, *Metamora, or, The Last of the Wampanoags* by J. A. Stone (Edward Callary, *Place Names of Illinois* [Urbana: University of Illinois, 2009]).

*Turn **right** (east) on IL 116, and go 0.5 miles to Menard Street. Turn **left** on Menard and park in front of the Metamora Courthouse.*

 The Courthouse Marker is located in front of the courthouse.

 This courthouse, built in 1845, and Mount Pulaski's are the only two Circuit courthouses still standing in their original locations. The first floor contains an informative museum, with exhibits related to the courthouse and other parts of Circuit. The museum displays artifacts from the Metamora House and the inn at the tiny village of Bowling Green. In front of the courthouse are two millstones from Panther Creek near the town site of Bowling Green, both of which you will visit on this tour.

Wayside Exhibit 5: "The Circuit Lawyer"
This exhibit across the street from the courthouse tells the story of Lincoln's 1857 defense of Melissa Goings, who was on trial for the murder of her abusive husband, Roswell. In self-defense, as Roswell assaulted her yet again, Melissa grabbed a piece of firewood and struck him with it, inadvertently killing him. The jury trial was not going well when Lincoln asked for a recess, and he took Melissa to an anteroom downstairs. When she asked him for a drink of water,

The courtroom of the Metamora Courthouse in which Lincoln practiced is on the second floor, maintained as it was when Lincoln walked that floor.

he told her that there was good water in the Tennessee River and then opened a window. Melissa escaped and was never seen again in Illinois. John McClarey's statue of Lincoln and Melissa stands next to the exhibit. The exhibit also provides further information about Lincoln's legal career in Woodford County.

Across the park on the east side of IL 116 is the site of Metamora House, the inn where the lawyers stayed. On September 22, 1851, David Davis wrote to his wife Sarah, "The tavern at Woodford is miserable. It may be that Mr. Cross may take compassion and take us to his house." Samuel Cross was the Circuit clerk, with whom Lincoln and Davis occasionally stayed.

*Return to IL 116 and proceed **left** (east) out of town 1.2 miles to Mennonite Road. Turn **right** (south) and proceed to a T intersection, Tazewood Road (C 29000 N), then turn **left** (east), proceed east, and bear **left** at the cemetery onto Mount Zion Road, which runs parallel to Walnut Creek. This is another of the authentic Lincoln roads that he took as he proceeded from Metamora to Walnut Grove and, ultimately, Bloomington. Follow this road to IL 117; turn **right** on IL 117 into Eureka.*

Metamora House.

TOWN OF EUREKA

Walnut Grove was incorporated as the Town of Eureka in 1855. Most of the residents were strong supporters of Lincoln, which was unique because the county as a whole was Democratic.

> *Proceed on IL 117 (Main Street) past the courthouse and past Reagan Drive to 4H Park Road. Turn **left** and proceed east 2.1 miles to C 1600 E. Go **right** (south) and drive 0.9 miles, then stop.*

The stone on the shoulder on the east side of the road commemorates the site of Versailles, the first county seat. Lincoln practiced here briefly before the county seat moved to Metamora. One of the conditions of that 1840 move was that a facility suitable for holding court be provided, so the county put the primitive courthouse on skids and pulled it to Metamora.

> *Pass the stone and turn **left** (east) on C 700 N. Proceed east on C 700 N. At the T intersection, turn **right** (south) and proceed one mile to a curve. Turn **right** and stay southbound, continuing to C 550 N. Go **right** (west), following 550 N to a T intersection (C 1915 E). Turn **right** (north) and follow the road to the east bank of Panther Creek.*

*Turn around and return 0.7 miles on 1915 E, past the T intersection,
and stop.*

This is the site of Bowling Green. To the west is the tavern where Lincoln
occasionally stayed and is said to have debated Peter Cartwright during their
1846 Congressional race. To the east of the road, back in the woods along the
ridge that runs northeast, is the town cemetery, whose gravestones date to the
1840s. The arrival of the Illinois Central Railroad caused the town's residents
to pick up and move to the hamlet of Kappa. A large stone a short distance
south on the right side of the road marks Bowling Green.

*The itinerant lawyers used this ford to cross Panther Creek, the principal tributary of the
Mackinaw River. This spot was also the site of a grist mill, whose stones are now in front of
the Metamora Courthouse.*

Letcher Basin, north of the Mackinaw River.

*Turn **left** and follow the road through a series of turns to C 1975 E. Turn **right** (south) and follow this road to a dead end overlooking Letcher Basin of the Mackinaw River.*

This road along the ridge, intact since Lincoln's time, is the actual road Lincoln used when he went through the basin and across the Mackinaw.

*Turn around and return to the T intersection at C 475 N, then turn **right** (east) to C 2000 E. Turn **left** (north) and proceed 1.2 miles to C 600 N. Turn **right** (east) and proceed 2.9 miles to C 2300 E. Turn **right** (south) and descend the hill across the Mackinaw River and up the hill to C 375 N. Turn **right** (west) on C 375 N, then make a sharp **left** followed by an immediate **right** (west) on C 355 N. Follow this winding road across Denman Creek, and you will eventually reach Denman Road. Proceed **right** (north) to the Mackinaw River and park in the ParkLands lot.*

You have arrived at Wyatt's Ford, used by Lincoln to cross the river.

*Turn around and follow Denman Road south to a stop sign and a cemetery on the **right**.*

This cemetery was started by the "Old Democrat" Abraham Carlock, for whom today's nearby town is named, and was intended by him to hold only the remains of those members of his party. According to a family account, Lincoln stopped to visit Carlock on occasion at his home in the vicinity, but the exact location of it is unknown.

Continue south toward the county line.

The Republican Cemetery is a short distance south on the east side of the road.

Proceed just beyond that cemetery to the next County Line Marker, on the right.

4 Woodford-McLean: The County Line Marker is located on the west side of the road (GPS: N 40°36'39.0", W 89°07'46.1").

2. HEADING SOUTH AND THEN EAST

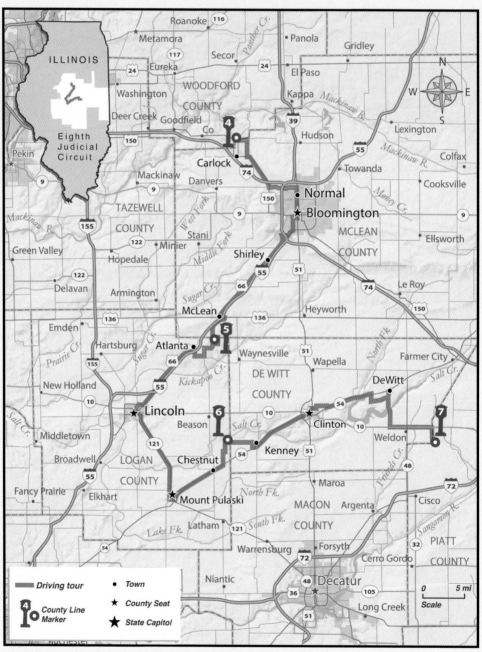

Map showing the north central part of the Circuit.

MCLEAN (BLOOMINGTON)

MCLEAN COUNTY WAS FORMED IN 1830 WITH BLOOMINGTON

as its seat, then a nonexistent town on the north edge of Blooming Grove, a 3,000-acre hardwood grove in which the county's first residents had settled. McLean County was one of only three counties to be part of the Eighth Judicial Circuit throughout the Circuit's existence. Lincoln spent more time in Bloomington than in any city other than Springfield. The most significant allies in his political rise were from Bloomington, including David Davis, Jesse Fell, Asahel Gridley, and Leonard Swett.

*Proceed south to C 2250 N, turn **left** (east) and proceed to C 2225 E; go **right** and proceed south to US 150. Turn **left** on US 150, proceed across I-74 to a traffic light (Raab Road); turn **left** on Raab and proceed east to Main Street in Normal.*

TOWN OF NORMAL

The Town of Normal was not founded until 1865, so Lincoln and his fellows would have continued south on what is now US 150 to Market Street and into Bloomington. Normal was known as North Bloomington at that time. It was the home of town founder Jesse Fell, who was one of Lincoln's most important advocates.

*Proceed south on Main and prepare to turn **left** on College Avenue. Turn **left** (east) and prepare to turn **right** on University Street. Turn **right** (south) and proceed one block to the next Wayside Exhibit, on the east side of the street across from Thomas Metcalf School.*

Wayside Exhibit 6: "Illinois State University"
McLean County, led by Fell and with the help of Lincoln as his attorney, successfully established Illinois State Normal University, the state's first public university.

*Proceed south to Beaufort Street. Turn **left** (east) on Beaufort Street to Broadway. Turn **right** (south) on Broadway and cross the tracks to park. On the median at the intersection of Broadway and Irving Street you will see Wayside Exhibit 7.*

Home of Jesse Fell.

🏃 Wayside Exhibit 7: "Jesse Fell Home / Lincoln and Fell"

Jesse Fell built his home upon this 18-acre site in 1856, a place Lincoln frequently visited.

Jesse Fell.

CITY OF BLOOMINGTON

*Proceed south on Broadway across Virginia Avenue, around the curve to Hillcrest Street and then **right** to Clinton Street. Take Clinton south to Locust Street. Drive **left** (east) on Locust to Linden Street/Woodruff Drive. Turn **right** on Woodruff, then veer **right** onto Linden and proceed south, noting the Davis Mansion on the **left**. Proceed to the David Davis Mansion site.*

David and Sarah Davis and daughter, Sally, and their first home at Clover Lawn. As Lincoln's campaign manager in 1860, Davis was perhaps the person most responsible for Lincoln's nomination. Sarah was also close to Lincoln.

🏃 Wayside Exhibit 8: "My Good Friend"

This exhibit is at the David Davis Mansion's Visitor Center. As the Circuit judge, Davis spent countless hours with Lincoln and was among his closest friends. This mansion was built in 1872 on the footprint of Davis's first home, where Lincoln frequently stayed. The barn was here in Lincoln's time, and it is probable that Lincoln kept his horse there. It contains an excellent exhibit on Lincoln and the Eighth Judicial Circuit titled *Prelude to the Presidency*.

*Leave the mansion by driving south on Davis Street to Washington Street. Take a **left** and then an immediate **right** on McClun Street, then continue south to Grove Street. Turn **right** (west) on Grove and proceed half a block to the Constitution Trail, once the Illinois Central Railroad.*

Asahel Gridley, client and political ally of Lincoln's. It is said that Gridley, Bloomington's first millionaire, spent $100,000 in support of Lincoln's campaigns.

🏃 Wayside Exhibit 9: "Illinois Central Railroad"

The Illinois Central Depot, shown in this exhibit on the north side of the street, stood on the west side of Constitution Trail and the north side of Grove Street. Lincoln occasionally took the train from Decatur to Bloomington, disembarked here, and walked to the Davis house.

Proceed west on Grove Street to 510 East Grove.

🎩 Reuben Benjamin, who was certified by Lincoln to practice law, lived here. Lincoln visited this home on occasion, which was built in 1857 by John Routt, county sheriff. Routt served on Grant's staff during the Civil War, was appointed by him as the last territorial governor of Colorado, and then became the state's first elected governor.

Proceed west on Grove across Gridley Street to Prairie Street.

Behind the large twentieth-century apartment building is "The Oaks," Gridley's home. Gridley was a successful lawyer who practiced frequently with and against Lincoln. His success in business allowed him to turn his law practice over to Lincoln, who thenceforth represented him. He arguably had the most impact on the growth and development of Bloomington. Lincoln first visited this grand home in 1859, which was built at a cost $40,000. Legend has it that the opulence of the home and perhaps Gridley's arrogance led Lincoln to say to his friend, "Gridley, do you want everybody to hate you?"

Continue west on Grove to East Street.

To the left at this intersection is the site of James Allin's store, the first building in what would become the City of Bloomington. Allin founded Bloomington, and Lincoln represented his son, James Allin Jr., in several matters, including a mortgage foreclosure against Stephen Douglas. Douglas defaulted, allowing judgment to be entered against him.

*Turn **right** on East and take the immediate **left** (Front Street). Park your car for a walking tour of downtown Bloomington, which will begin at the courthouse square, a block north of Front at the intersection of Main and Washington. Main is one block west of East, and Washington is one block north of Front.*

Walking Tour of Downtown Bloomington

The Courthouse Square and the blocks in the immediate area to the south feature fourteen buildings that date back to the Lincoln era. He entered at least seven of them for certain and probably the others as well at one time or another.

McLean County Courthouse, in which Lincoln practiced throughout his career.

■ This courthouse stood from 1836 to 1868. It was of the coffee mill design, so called because of its shape. It was built by Leander Munsell of Paris, Illinois. The building you now see served as the courthouse from 1904 to 1976 and is currently the McLean County Museum of History.

Proceed to the McLean County Museum of History.

▮ Note the Courthouse Marker on the east side of the building. Proceed to the south side of the building where you will see a statue of a seated Lincoln by Rick Harney. Enter the south entrance of the Museum's Visitor Center to see the exhibit "Cruising with Lincoln on 66." An interactive exhibit titled "Abraham Lincoln in McLean County," which opened in 2016, is located on the level above the entry floor.

*Exit the museum's south entrance and walk **left** (east) to the southeast corner of the courthouse square.*

🏃 Wayside Exhibit 10: "The Phoenix Block"
The Phoenix Block is so named because it was built upon the ashes of the devastating fire of 1855, which destroyed much of the block, including the National Hotel. The exhibit tells of a medical malpractice case that Lincoln defended, known as the "Chicken Bone Case," in which he represented Dr. Eli Crothers. During the fire, a spectator named Fleming fractured both legs when a portion of the National Hotel collapsed on him. Crothers performed successful surgery on one leg, but the procedure was less so on the other. Leonard Swett filed a malpractice suit. In his closing argument, Lincoln used bones from an old chicken and a young chicken to demonstrate that the unsuccessful surgery was due to the brittleness of the man's aging bones. The trial resulted in a hung jury, and the case was later settled out of court.

Cross Main to the northeast corner of the intersection of Main and Washington.

🏃 Wayside Exhibit 11: "Lincoln the Lawyer"
Lincoln's stature grew substantially as a lawyer during his 23 years in Bloomington. His very first client, John W. Baddeley, fired him because of his obvious inexperience and his callow and rustic manner. This contrasts sharply with Lincoln's most significant case, *Illinois Central Railroad vs. McLean*

County, Illinois, and Parke. As a means of subsidizing construction of the railroads, the legislature exempted railroad lands from real estate taxes, which was a principle source of revenue for the counties. In 1853 Lincoln filed suit for the Illinois Central Railroad seeking to enjoin McLean County from collecting this tax. The county contended that the exemption was unconstitutional special legislation. Lincoln won the case in the trial court and ultimately in the Supreme Court in 1857. He charged his client $5,000 (approximately $116,000 today), by far the largest fee of his career. He had to sue the railroad in McLean County to get paid. He later estimated that he had saved the railroad half a million dollars in taxes ($11.5 million today).

The "Indignation Meeting," held on the square on Easter Sunday, April 16, 1865, to mourn Lincoln's assassination, is also described here.

Proceed across Washington and continue south to the southeast corner of Front and Main.

 Wayside Exhibit 12: "Miller-Davis Building and Asahel Gridley's Bank"
Numerous lawyers practiced in the Miller-Davis Building, including Lincoln, David Davis, Asahel Gridley, John M. Scott, and Davis's partner, Wells Colton. The building was built in 1843 and is the oldest commercial building in the city. The exhibit's reverse side includes a picture of the McLean County Bank, the building that still stands across Main, which Lincoln visited often. Gridley's owned the bank, the county's first, and the telegraph office, both located in that building. He also owned the gas company, which he obtained with Lincoln's legal help. Lincoln represented him on numerous matters, including the slander case *Flagg vs. Gridley.* Lincoln's defense was that pejorative words uttered by Gridley were not slander because he said such things about everybody.

Proceed across Front to the lobby of the Law and Justice Center.

A statue of Lincoln by Keith Knoblock, titled *A. Lincoln—Circuit Lawyer,* stands in the lobby.

Cross back over Front to the northwest corner of Front and Main by the Gridley building. Walk west on Front.

This block, known as the "Rounds Block," was constructed in 1857 following the fire two years earlier.

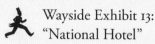

Wayside Exhibit 13:
"National Hotel"

This exhibit tells the story of Lincoln's connection to the 33-room National Hotel built on this site, which was destroyed by the 1855 fire and from which Lincoln's "Chicken Bone" case arose (see Wayside Exhibit 10).

Continue west to Center Street, turn right and proceed north across the alley.

Leonard Swett, one of Lincoln's closest friends and David Davis's chief lieutenant. Swett, a native of Maine, came here after serving in the Mexican War and became one of the Circuit's leading trial lawyers.

The building on the north side of the alley is where Lincoln delivered a nonpolitical lecture titled "Discovery and Inventions" on April 6, 1858, while here for the spring court session. The lecture took place in Centre Hall, located at the south end of the third floor. The large doorway you see provided access to the hall for Lincoln and his audience that night. This is the Crothers Building, owned by Lincoln's client, Dr. Eli Crothers. Lincoln visited this building frequently, and many of his law-practicing contemporaries, including Ward Hill Lamon, Leonard Swett, William Ward Orme, and Harvey Hogg, had offices in this building and the one adjacent to the east.

Look back across Washington Street to the southeast and compare the scene pictured with the Phoenix Block of today. Note the buildings still standing. The Bloomington Pantagraph *was published on the upper floors of 210 N. Center Street, another office frequently visited by Lincoln. The* Pantagraph *is still published nearby.*

Cross Center, then Washington, and walk to 210 N. Center.

Walk south on Center across Jefferson Street, then cross to the other side of Center and walk south to the southeast corner of Center and Monroe Street.

🏃 Wayside Exhibit 14: "Pike House"

The Pike House, the prominent hotel from whose balcony Lincoln delivered a speech on May 28, 1856, formerly stood on this site. Lincoln was a frequent guest at the Pike House, as were many notable visitors to Bloomington, including Stephen A. Douglas.

Return across Jefferson and Washington to the southeast corner of Washington and Center. Then walk east on Washington to the center of the block.

🎩 On April 10, 1860, here at Phoenix Hall while in town for his final court session, Lincoln gave his last speech before his presidential nomination a month later. The speech included his standard antislave content.

Continue east to the southwest corner of Main and Washington. Stop at 111 E. Washington.

Pike House.

The law office of Kersey Fell, brother of Jesse, was on the second floor of 111 E. Washington. Lincoln used this office on occasion.

This marks the end of your walking tour.

Drive north on Main to the southwest corner of Main and Locust Street.

Wayside Exhibit 15: "William Florville"
William Florville of Springfield, Lincoln's Haitian barber, purchased property at this location. When the Bloomington developers of this lot refused to honor their contract with Florville to sell him the lot, Lincoln threatened a lawsuit on Florville's behalf to enforce their agreement. The developers relented and conveyed the lot to Florville.

Park and carefully walk across East/Main Street to the statue of Abraham Lincoln, David Davis, and Jesse Fell in front of the Center for Performing Arts.

William Florville, a resident of both Springfield and Bloomington, and Lincoln's client.

This narrative statue by Andrew Jumonville titled *Convergence of Purpose* tells how the lives of David Davis, Jesse Fell, and Lincoln converged in 1860, culminating with Lincoln's nomination for president and Bloomington's place in this story.

Drive north on Main to Chestnut. Turn left on Chestnut and proceed west all the way to the railroad tracks.

Lincoln frequently passed through the Chicago and Alton Train Station as he traveled between Springfield and Chicago, as well as to Bloomington. The incoming railroads increased Lincoln's mobility, aiding in his law practice and politics. His last appearance here was on November 21, 1860, on his way to Chicago to meet his vice president–elect, Hannibal Hamlin, for the first time. He gave a brief speech from the back of the train.

On May 3, 1865, Lincoln's funeral train, also bearing the body of his son, Willie, who had died in 1862, passed through at 5:00 A.M. as a crowd of 8,000 waited to pay their last respects.

*Return east on Chestnut to Center, then turn **right** and go south to Locust. Turn **left** (east) on Locust and proceed to McLean Street. Turn **right** (south) on McLean and go to the northwest corner of the intersection of Jefferson and McLean.*

Wayside Exhibit 16: "Lincoln's Real Estate"
Lincoln purchased a lot here in 1852 for $325, with no known reason for doing so. He sold it in 1856 for $400.
This completes the Lincoln tour in Bloomington-Normal.
Lincoln would leave McLean County and proceed to Logan County.

*Return to E. Washington Street, then go west to S. Morris Avenue. Turn **left** (south) and proceed to Veterans Parkway. Turn **right** (south) and go to Foxcreek Road. Turn **right** (west) on Foxcreek to S. Beich Road, which becomes Historic Route 66 and runs parallel to I-55. Turn **left** and proceed south on Route 66, which also runs parallel to the tracks, and continue south into McLean.*

These tracks are the same ones that Lincoln traveled when he rode the Chicago and Alton line. The road enters Funks Grove, whose oaks witnessed Lincoln's passage. His friend, client, and patriarch of the prominent Funk family, Isaac, lived nearby, and Lincoln would occasionally visit him.

*Proceed into McLean to Main Street. Turn **left** on Main and proceed to US 136. Turn **left** (east) on US 136 (Dixie Road) and pass under I-55 to the first southbound country road (C 575 E), then turn **right** (south) and proceed three miles to a road intersecting from the east (C 1580 E). Turn **left**, proceed 0.3 miles, then stop.*

McLean-Logan: This Marker on the south side of the road is set in the center of the actual location of the Lincoln Circuit north-south road, then known as the Stage Coach Road. The original plaque was stolen, but it was replaced by Paul Adams of Atlanta (GPS: N 40°16'54.7", W 89°10'52.3").

LOGAN: PART 2 (POSTVILLE, MT. PULASKI, AND LINCOLN)

THE COUNTY WAS FIRST SETTLED IN 1819 NEAR PRESENT-DAY

Elkhart, which was then northern Sangamon County. Lincoln, the legislator, drafted Logan's boundaries and named it for John Logan, a Democrat from southern Illinois who had supported Lincoln's bill to move the state capital to Springfield two years earlier. Lincoln dominates the early history of Logan County. He performed surveys there, represented the area in his four terms in the legislature, and was the legislative leader in the county's formation. He had an active practice in Logan County and represented it in the litigation generated by the two moves of its seat. He was an attorney for the founders of the Town of Lincoln and engineered its designation as the county seat.

*Proceed east from the Marker to the next road (C 2500 Street / C 500 E), turn **right** (south), and proceed to an unmarked T intersection (C 2400 N). Turn **right** (east) and proceed 0.7 miles to an unmarked southbound gravel road and stop.*

The north-south road noted at the McLean-Logan County Line Marker continues south and then west.

On the southwest corner of the intersection stood the Halfway House, an inn operated by Samuel Hoblit, an 1828 settler. It was a two-story, framed building on the west side of the Stage Coach Road. Lincoln stayed at the inn and became friends with Hoblit's son John. Down the road to the left (south) is the Roach Chapel Cemetery, which was there when Lincoln passed. The following directions cross Clear Creek, where John Todd Stuart recalled that he and Lincoln fished while staying at the Halfway House.

*Continue west down the hill and turn **left**, proceeding south on C 2200 AV across Clear Creek.*

The Stage Coach Road in Lincoln's time continued south, and before reaching the cemetery, it headed in a southwesterly direction across the creek. A short distance after the turn to the south, the present road continues on a remnant of the old road, which the lawyers took across the creek.

Prior to the construction of the railroads, the Stage Coach Road proceeded south and east, dropping down to cross the Kickapoo Creek at a ford described as a "Missouri Crossing." The old road remains visible but is on private property.

*Proceed south to the T intersection, turn **right** on C 2350 ST, and go 0.8 miles west to C 2100 AV. Turn **right** and proceed around the curve, continuing west to I-55. Enter I-55 heading south.*

TOWN OF ATLANTA

Lincoln frequently visited Atlanta, a town created by the coming of the railroads in 1853. He had good clients in the town, including its founder Richard Gill as well as the Hoblit family. You are encouraged to visit Atlanta, whose sites are particularly important to Lincoln's political rise in the 1850s but are not directly related to his legal career.

When John Hoblit grew up and acquired his own farm, he lived with his family a short distance to the east of I-55, now marked by a row of steel grain storage bins. While traveling the Circuit, Lincoln occasionally

The traveling lawyers viewed this vista, virtually nothing but tall grass prairie, as they came off the Shelbyville Moraine. Note Elkhart Hill looming in the distance—23 miles to the southeast—owned by John Dean Gillett, a client and supporter of Lincoln and whose home Lincoln visited.

stayed with the Hoblits. In 1858, he spent the night in a shed there with John and his family, whose home had been destroyed by fire.

*Follow I-55 to the first Lincoln exit (Exit 133). The exit ramp takes you to US 66. Turn **left** (south) and follow US 66 around a curve to the west to Nicholson Road. Turn **left** (south) and proceed on Nicholson to the Lincoln College Campus and the Lincoln Heritage Museum. Park there.*

TOWN OF LINCOLN

The railroad from Alton to Chicago reached Logan County in 1853. Three real estate speculators, John Dean Gillett, Robert Latham, and Virgil Hickox, aided by their lawyer, Lincoln, devised a scheme by which a new town, as yet unnamed, would become county seat. They purchased land where the trains would have to stop for water. Lincoln's task was to pass a bill through the legislature, providing for a referendum to move the county seat from Mt. Pulaski to the yet unnamed town. On August 24 the three clients met in Lincoln's office, where he urged them to name this town before the impending sale of lots platted on the land they had purchased. They suggested "Lincoln," to which he reluctantly agreed. Three months after the successful lot sales, the referendum moving the county seat to Lincoln passed.

Lincoln College was established in 1865. Its founder, Robert Latham, wrote Lincoln on March 4 that year, detailing the growth of the town and informing him of his namesake college. Unfortunately, circumstances did not allow the busy president time to respond. The college's Lincoln Heritage Museum opened in 1942 and moved to its new location in 2014, offering a fresh examination of Lincoln's time in Illinois with artifacts and state-of-the-art exhibits using character voices to tell the Lincoln story. In front of the museum stands *Lincoln on the Move*, a statue of Lincoln reading, by Andrew Jumonville.

Upon leaving the museum, proceed around the curve where Nicholson Road becomes Ottawa Street. Follow Ottawa south to Keokuk Street.

A statue by Merrell Gage of a seated Lincoln appears to the right at this intersection.

*Cross Keokuk to Broadway and turn **left** on Broadway. Cross the tracks to Chicago Street and turn **left**, then stop.*

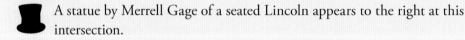

On the left is the old depot where Lincoln christened the new town on the day of the lot sales with the juice of a watermelon. The tracks from Alton had only reached this far by that date. Lincoln last visited the town on November 21, 1860, on his way to Chicago, and he spoke from the back of the train. On May 3, 1865, at 7:00 A.M., the Lincoln funeral train stopped briefly. Signs at this site tell the full story.

The Lincoln Hotel, where Lincoln passed the time on its broad porch while in town for court appearances, was located on the southeast corner of the intersection of Kickapoo and Broadway.

*Proceed north on Chicago to Pekin Street. Turn **right** (east) on Pekin and proceed one block to Kickapoo Street, then turn **right** on Kickapoo and proceed south. Park near the Logan County Courthouse.*

A Courthouse Marker appears on the west side of the courthouse. The statue at the southwest corner of the courthouse also contains a storyboard commemorating Lincoln's speech of October 16, 1858, during the Douglas campaign. The statue by David Seagraves was dedicated in 2015.

The Logan County Courthouse was built on this site in 1857 after the previous building was destroyed by a fire of questionable origin. Lincoln practiced in this building, which stood until 1907.

Samuel Parks, an attorney who frequently opposed but also associated with Lincoln, was a steadfast supporter of Lincoln from the time he was in Congress through his presidency. A native of Vermont, Parks came to Mt. Pulaski before moving to Lincoln. His office was across Kickapoo Street, west of the courthouse. Lincoln appointed him to the Supreme Court of the Idaho Territory.

*Proceed past the courthouse and turn **left** on Pulaski, then proceed one-half block.*

Lincoln took two lots at this location from James Primm, one of Postville's founders, as payment of a $400 loan that Lincoln made to Primm.

*Proceed around the square, west on Broadway to Logan Street. Turn **left** (south) and proceed around a curve to Fifth Street. Proceed west on Fifth Street to the site of the Postville Courthouse. Drive around the square and park.*

This is the site of the first Logan County seat. Postville was a tiny hamlet of less than 100 people, surrounded by prairie, and chosen because it occupied a central location in the county. Lincoln is said to have played town ball, a primitive form of baseball, between court cases here. The courthouse was built in 1840 and was

Postville Courthouse.

used until 1847. It was neglected over the years and became badly dilapidated, and it was purchased by Henry Ford in 1929 and moved to Greenfield Village in Dearborn, Michigan. The state erected this replica in 1953.

A historical Marker at the VFW across the street marks the location of Deskins's Tavern, where visitors—including Circuit-riding lawyers, witnesses, and litigants—stayed while court was in session. The first Circuit court session in the county was held in the tavern before the courthouse was completed. The pump on the corner in the front connects to the well that serviced the tavern.

Lincoln recounted this story from his Postville days. A weary traveler arrived late one night at Deskins's Tavern seeking a room. The tavern keeper advised the man that there was no vacancy. The disappointed traveler asked if he could buy a whiskey. The innkeeper advised him that he was out of whiskey. The disgruntled rider replied, "Well, then can you bring me a cup of water and a cob of corn and I'll make my own." Lincoln used this story to respond to Union generals who constantly complained of their lack of resources.

*Return on Fifth to Logan and proceed to Broadway. Proceed **right** (southeast) on Broadway to IL 121. Turn **right** and travel to Mt. Pulaski; after crossing Deer and Salt Creeks, enter Mt. Pulaski, going straight on Vine Street, and continue south to E. Jefferson Street. Turn **right** and proceed to the Mt. Pulaski Courthouse and Square.*

TOWN OF MT. PULASKI

Settled in 1836, Mt. Pulaski sits on a 60-foot glacial kame. Citizens of the town contributed $2,700 toward the construction of the Greek revival courthouse to attract the county seat from Postville. They succeeded in 1847 but lost the seat in 1853 when it moved to Lincoln. Each move of the county seat resulted in a suit by the residents of the rejected town against Logan County. Lincoln successfully defended the county in both cases.

Wayside Exhibit 17: "Circuit Court Stop / Lincoln's Law Practice"
This exhibit describes two of Lincoln's cases in Mt. Pulaski, both of which involved patents, an uncommon subject of litigation. In one, Lincoln defended a claim that his client had fraudulently misrepresented the nature of a "cast iron tombstone" patent to investors. Lincoln lost the case in the trial

The Mt. Pulaski Courthouse and Metamora are the only two court-houses in which Lincoln practiced that still stand on their original sites. The Courthouse Marker is visible in the foreground.

court, but the result was reversed in the Supreme Court and remanded for further proceedings. In the other, Lincoln represented an investor who was also seeking to recover money because of misrepresentation of a patent, this time for a mechanical "horological cradle" that rocked itself. When Lincoln demonstrated the cradle in court, he couldn't shut it off, which caused Judge Davis to remark that it reminded him of many lawyers who could not stop talking once they got started.

A Courthouse Marker stands on the south side of the courthouse. Logan is the only county with two Markers; both were erected to resolve the dispute over which town should have a Courthouse Marker.

Leave the square on the north side by going west to the 100 block of Marion Street; the site of the Thomas Lushbaugh House is on the west side of the street.

Lincoln and Davis occasionally stayed at the home of Thomas Lush-baugh, a former neighbor of Lincoln's in Springfield, because of the poor accommodations at the Mt. Pulaski House.

Interior of the Mt. Pulaski courtroom.

*Return to the west side of the square and proceed from the square south on Washington to McDonald Street. Turn **left** (east) on McDonald and cross IL 121 to US 54. Turn **left** on US 54, proceeding north, then east 6.9 miles to C 2300 E. Turn **left** (north) and proceed to C 1150 ST. Go **right** (east) 0.2 miles to C 2325 AV. Turn **left** (north) and proceed 0.9 miles to the first **right**, C 12 N; go **right** (east) 0.7 miles and stop.*

The lawyers usually stayed at the Mt. Pulaski House, notorious for its poor accommodations. David Davis called it "perhaps the hardest place you ever saw. . . . everything is dirty and eating terrible." It stood on the northwest corner across the street from the courthouse.

6 Logan-DeWitt: The Marker is on the north side of the road at the northeast corner of the intersection (GPS: N 40°0.6'0.1", W 89°0.8'40.6") and is
missing its top.

DEWITT (CLINTON)

THE AREA THAT WOULD BECOME DEWITT COUNTY WAS FIRST

settled in 1824. Lincoln's Bloomington friends James Allin and Jesse Fell
were returning to Bloomington from Decatur in 1835 when they stopped at
a gradual hill. They decided it would be a good location for a town, which
became the spot where Clinton was founded. In order to spur growth and
the sale of lots, Allin, a state senator, pushed a bill through the legislature in
1839 creating DeWitt County out of part of Macon County to the south and
McLean County to the north. The county and its seat were named for Governor DeWitt Clinton of New York. Clinton boomed with the formation of the
county, which was followed by a referendum that selected Clinton over Marion (now the town of DeWitt) as county seat. This county was in the Eighth
Judicial Circuit from its formation throughout Lincoln's career and played
an important role in Lincoln's rise. He practiced in the county before there
were any local lawyers and continued until he ran for the presidency. His last
court session here was in October 1859. His caseload included a substantial
amount of litigation for the Illinois Central Railroad, often involving damage
to property neighboring the railroad right of way during its construction. The
community's animosity toward the railroad never spilled over onto Lincoln.

*Proceed east from the Marker into Kenney (3.1 miles), turn **right** on Johnson
Street, and proceed south through Kenney to IL 54. Turn **left** (east) on IL 54
and drive to Clinton.*

IL 54 runs parallel to Salt Creek, which the road crosses before reaching Clinton. Lincoln likely would have followed this route from Mt.
Pulaski to Clinton.

*Continue east across US 51 into Clinton. Proceed across Business 51 to
Center Street. Turn **left** on Center (north) toward what had been the
courthouse square. Proceed to the intersection of Center and Adams Street.
Park in the parking lot located at the southeast corner, and walk toward
the courthouse square.*

TOWN OF CLINTON

Walking Tour of Downtown Clinton and Lincoln's Square

🏃 Wayside Exhibit 18: "Humorous Moment"

This exhibit tells a story of Lincoln the practical joker. As a boy was tying up Lincoln's horse in front of the Barnett Tavern, Lincoln told him that the desk clerk in the tavern was deaf. Lincoln then went inside and told the same thing to the desk clerk about the boy. When the boy and the desk clerk finally communicated with each other, they did so at an extraordinarily high volume.

This exhibit also describes the Barnett House, the tavern where Lincoln and the lawyers spent much of their time during court week in Clinton. It formerly stood at the parking lot south of Adams.

🎩 While standing at this exhibit, look across the street at the Moore and Warner building at the northwest corner of the intersection. This building was Clifton Moore's office and is still occupied by his descendants. Lincoln practiced law here while in Clinton. Moore was the county's first attorney; his descendants are still influential in the affairs of the town. Attorney Lawrence Weldon arrived in Clinton shortly after Moore. Both of them handled many cases with and against Lincoln and were among his staunchest political supporters. Lincoln was a frequent visitor for both politics and law.

Walk across Center and proceed north to the next Wayside Exhibit, located before you reach the square.

🏃 Wayside Exhibit 19: "Lincoln's Friends and Foes"

Lincoln had an unusual relationship with the eccentric and erratic Thomas Snell, a Clinton resident who became a millionaire as a contractor laying track for the Illinois Central Railroad. Lincoln's client, Jeremiah Kelly, gave six 50-dollar promissory notes to Snell to cover wagers on the 1852 presidential election, which Kelly then refused to pay. Represented by Lawrence Weldon, Snell sued to recover on the notes. Lincoln and Moore contended the notes were illegal and void. The court ruled for Snell.

Cross the street and enter the square.

The courthouse square with its seven buildings from the Lincoln period has an aura of that time as the traveler scans the scene. There are a number of Lincoln sites around the square, some of which are related to politics and not the law.

 You will see a Courthouse Marker on the southeast edge of the square.

 Wayside Exhibit 20: "Lincoln at Work and Play"

This exhibit describes Lincoln's 20-year association with DeWitt County, which began with his first court session in October 1839 and included most of the circuit court sessions until his last one in 1859. Lincoln would relax between court sessions by learning billiards at a parlor in Clinton and long jumping.

Walk north one block across to the northwest corner of Washington and Center. The adjacent county building replaced the late nineteenth-century courthouse that previously stood on the square.

This courthouse in which Lincoln practiced was built in 1841, replacing an 1839 frame building.

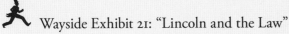

Wayside Exhibit 21: "Lincoln and the Law"

This exhibit tells of two DeWitt County cases. In the first, illuminating the racism of the day, Lincoln's client sued another man for slander, claiming that the defendant had spread the rumor that the plaintiff was "a Negro." His case was successful, and he recovered a judgment in the amount of $737.50. In the other case, Lincoln and Stephen A. Douglas teamed up to triumphantly defend the County's first murder charge. Lincoln had to sue to recover his fee.

Walk north two blocks to the north end of the Vespasian Warner Library on Johnson Street.

Wayside Exhibit 22: "Lawyers and Book Lovers—Warner Memories"

The library contains the vast book collection of Clifton Moore and his son-in-law, Vespasian Warner. Moore was an obsessive collector of books, and Lincoln frequently used this extensive library.

At the northwest corner of Johnson and Center, a large stone marks the site of the hill where the town's founders, "Allen" [*sic*] and Fell, stopped in 1835. This ends your walking tour.

*Return to the parking lot; proceed in your car to the square. Go **right** (east) from the square on Main Street to Railroad Avenue.*

For two blocks south of Main Street, the land east of Railroad Avenue once belonged to Alexander Argo, whose home Lincoln visited on occasion. In 1850, Lincoln represented Argo in defense of a lien that had been placed against Argo's property. The case was settled. Seven years later, a client of Lincoln's named Cross sued Argo for negligent operation of his wagon, which resulted in a collision injuring Cross. Lincoln recovered a verdict of $37.08.

*Turn around and turn **left** (west) on Main to the square and then to Center. Turn **right** (north) on Center through town to Woodlawn Street. Turn **right** on Woodlawn and proceed to the Clifton Moore Homestead and DeWitt County Museum. Enter the parking lot in order to visit the mansion.*

Wayside Exhibit 23: "Friends to the End"

Lincoln had a close relationship with Clifton Moore, who purchased this mansion—known as the Homestead—in 1880. This is now the DeWitt County History Museum, which includes Moore's spectacular library. A balcony circles the entire two-story room.

Clifton Moore, the county's first millionaire, was a close friend and real estate partner of David Davis.

Leave the Homestead and proceed **left** (east) under the viaduct to Cain Street (a T intersection). Turn **left** (north), then turn **right** (east) on Marion Street and proceed 0.2 miles to the first Clifton Moore house.

Wayside Exhibit 24: "On the Campaign Trail"

Before purchasing the Homestead, Moore constructed this home on 80 acres of land he had purchased from David Davis, and Lincoln stayed here on occasion.

Proceed east to the T intersection (C 11500 E, Reagan Road) and turn **right** (south) to IL 54. Turn **left** (east) on IL 54 and proceed 5.5 miles to Wren Road, C 16750 E. Turn **right** and proceed south 0.8 miles. At the first intersection (C 8110 N) turn **left** and proceed north on DeWitt Road (Old Clinton Road) to the T intersection in the town of DeWitt. Turn **left** on Chicago Street and go north one block to the square (Springfield Street). Turn **right** on Springfield. You are now on the square.

Wayside Exhibit 25: "Whiskey Mayhem—the Law and Lodging"

This exhibit tells the story of the breakup of the town tavern by a band of nine female temperance advocates in 1854. The women were the wives of some of the town's leading businessmen. Lincoln, referring to the case as "People vs Mr. Whiskey", unsuccessfully defended the women against charges of criminal damage to property in *People vs. Shurtleff*. Each was fined two dollars. The exhibit also describes the Richter Boarding House where Judge Davis, Lincoln, and others stayed as they traveled between Clinton and Monticello. You will see the "square" that was intended for the courthouse if the town had been selected as county seat.

*Proceed **left** on Bloomington Street, around the square past the tavern at the southeast corner, which was the site of the tavern in the Shurtleff case. Continue around the square, **left** on Market Street to the northwest corner, the site of the Richter House.*

*Turn **left** on Chicago and drive south out of town to IL 10. Turn **left** (east) on IL 10 and proceed five miles to C 24000 E, Sunnyland Road, then turn **right** (south) on C 24000 E and travel two miles to the next Marker.*

7 DeWitt-Piatt: The Marker is on the east side of the road (GPS: N 40°05'58.8", W 58°41'15.8 "). The farm across the road was purchased by David Davis from the Illinois Central Railroad and is still owned by his descendants.

3. CONTINUING EAST AND THEN HEADING SOUTH

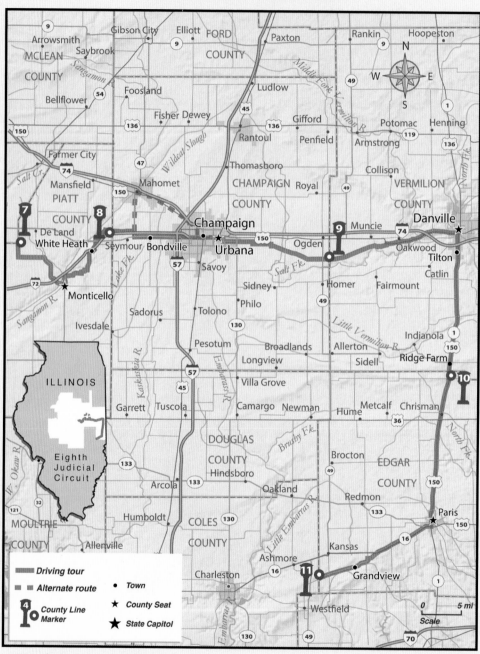

Map showing the east side of the Circuit.

PIATT (MONTICELLO)

PIATT COUNTY, ESTABLISHED IN 1841 FROM PORTIONS OF

DeWitt and Macon Counties, was part of the Circuit until 1853. Because it was the smallest county in the Circuit in both area and population, court sessions were brief and Lincoln's volume of business here was light.

*Turn **left** (east) at the Marker (C 2100 N) and proceed one mile to C 400 E Drive. Turn **left** (north) and proceed for one-half mile, then turn **right** (east) on C 2150 N and proceed 1.2 miles to DeLand-Monticello Road (no number). Turn **right** (south) and proceed around a series of curves into Monticello, crossing the Sangamon River. The lawyers entered Monticello by this route.*

The lawyers crossed the Sangamon here on a primitive ferry, which operated before a bridge was built. David Davis once swam his horses across instead of waiting for the ferryman, then transported his carriage across on the ferryman's canoe.

TOWN OF MONTICELLO

Monticello was founded and platted in 1830 by James Piatt, for whom the county is named, and it has been the county seat ever since.

*Proceed east on Bridge Street through the stoplight to N. State Street. Turn **right** on N. State, cross the tracks, and enter the parking lot to the **left** behind the former Allerton Library at the Depot/Tourist Information Center.*

Wayside Exhibit 26: "Monticello Journeys"

Several anecdotes of Lincoln's time in Monticello survive. For example, Ezra Marquis and Robert Guy, prominent local Republicans, were the only people to meet Lincoln on September 17, 1856, as he campaigned for John C. Frémont. Others include the story of Davis crossing the Sangamon and the axe-throwing contest, both of which are described elsewhere in this section.

*Return to N. State and go **left** (south) to E. Livingston Street. Turn **right** (west) on E. Livingston and proceed to N. Charter Street. Turn **left** (south) on N. Charter and proceed across W. Washington Street to the Courthouse Marker located in the middle of the block.*

The first Piatt County Courthouse, a simple, one-story, frame building constructed in 1845 was moved to the west side of the square in 1856 when the second courthouse was built.

You will find a Courthouse Marker in the lawn behind the courthouse.

Continue south and stop at the corner of Charter and Main Street.

In front of the southwest corner where now stands the Preferred State Bank, Lincoln and Monticello lawyer John McDougal held a contest to see who could throw a butcher's axe the farthest. They stood in Charter Street and threw roughly the same distance in their warmups. Then in the actual contest, McDougal threw first, about the same distance. Then Lincoln threw the axe into a branch of Lizard Run at the bottom of the hill south of the current location of the Presbyterian Church, a distance of well over 100 feet. Another account tells that they threw west into the creek that once curved north there. Neither creek remains. McDougal chastised Lincoln for not warning him in advance that he could throw an axe so far.

*Turn **left** (east) on Main and proceed across State Street, stopping at the southeast corner.*

Wayside Exhibit 27: "Lincoln in Monticello"

Once, when Lincoln was staying at the Tenbrook Hotel, he encouraged some children playing with an inflated pig bladder to throw it into the fire. It exploded, and while Lincoln hastened to clean up the mess, the broom he was using also caught fire. Fortunately the minor blaze was extinguished with no resultant damage.

*Continue east on Main Street to Independence Street, and turn **left** (north) to E. Washington Street. Turn **left** (west) on E. Washington and proceed to 200 W. Washington Street.*

The building known as the "Old Fort" stood at this location. Lincoln attended court in Old Fort until the construction of the first courthouse on the square.

On the right is the Tenbrook Hotel, where Lincoln and his fellow lawyers usually stayed. The hotel sat on the southwest corner of State and Main.

*Proceed west to Market Street, which is IL 105. Turn **right** on Market and proceed north approximately 1.2 miles to C 1730 N, which intersects IL 105 from the east. Proceed on the curving road 2.2 miles to another T intersection, C 1125 E. Turn **left** and proceed 0.2 to C 1780 N. Then go east around a curve to the **right** to C 1160 E, a distance of 0.3 miles, and drive north 0.1 miles to C 1800 N. Turn **right** and proceed 0.4 miles to C 1200 E to the Village of Whiteheath and a stop sign at IL 47 and adjacent to High Street. Proceed **right** on IL 47 (Mead Street) 0.7 miles, to the first **left** turn (C 1275E). Turn **left** and proceed over I-72, continuing north across IL 10 (C 2150 N). Take an immediate **right** at Ingram Cemetery, Wagon Trail Road, and go to the T intersection at C 2250 N. Turn **right** (east) and proceed through a series of four curves, where you will turn **right**, then immediately **left** (east). Follow this stretch of road 0.5 miles to an unmarked intersection. The next County Line Marker is on the **right**.*

8 Piatt-Champaign: This Marker is at the southwest corner of the unmarked intersection (GPS: N 40°07'28.5", W 88°27'47.2").

CHAMPAIGN (URBANA)

CHAMPAIGN COUNTY WAS FIRST SETTLED IN 1822. IT WAS

formally organized in 1833 from the western portion of Vermilion County, known as the "attached part of that county." The closest thing to a settlement was a small group of cabins in a timber known as the "Big Grove." However, that settlement was ignored in choosing a county seat. An unsettled tract south of Big Grove was designated as the new county seat and named Urbana (after Urbana in Champaign County, Ohio). Lots were sold in 1834 with such limited success that another sale was necessary a year later. Until the railroads came in 1854, Champaign's population was the smallest of any county, except for Piatt. It became part of the Eighth Judicial Circuit in 1841 and remained so throughout the balance of Lincoln's practice.

*Proceed east from the County Line Marker 0.5 miles to C 50 E. Turn **left** (north) and go 1.5 miles to a stone wall, then stop.*

 Lincoln frequently stopped here and sat on the porch with Harris, enjoying the panoramic view. Harris visited Lincoln early in his first

Behind this stone wall on top of the hill stood the grand home of Benjamin F. Harris, which was demolished in 2005.

year in the White House. The bed in
which Lincoln slept while staying at
Harris's home still belongs to the
owner of the property.

*Turn around and return south to C
1675 N. Turn **left** (east) and proceed
in an easterly direction to IL 47.*

At this point you have two choices.

ALTERNATE A: INTO CHAMPAIGN

The Circuit lawyers would have continued east to Urbana. Those directions are as follows:

*Turn **right** on IL 47 and proceed to
I-72. Go east on I-72 into Champaign. You will be on University
Street. If you have taken Alternate A,
skip the text to the subheading "City
of Champaign" on p. 60.*

*Harris, a colorful character and friend
of Lincoln's, made a fortune in land
speculation, and he raised cattle on his
property. He moved his first residence,
a log cabin, to its present location on
the east side of the driveway, east of the
location of the demolished big house.*

ALTERNATE B: TO MAHOMET'S MUSEUM OF THE GRANT PRAIRIE

*Turn **left** on IL 47 and proceed east through Mahomet, across I-74 to
the Museum.*

The Museum of the Grand Prairie presents an excellent exhibit about
the Circuit, including maps, films, and a life-size re-creation of several
Champaign County Lincoln sites, including the Goose Pond Church. The
Museum has two Wayside Exhibits.

Wayside Exhibit 28: "Champaign County's Lincoln"
The exhibit tells of Lincoln's Circuit travels and discusses his law practice
generally, which included numerous cases for the Illinois Central Railroad. It
also tells the story of the county's first murder case, *People vs. Weaver*. Lincoln

and Asahel Gridley's client, William Weaver, was convicted and sentenced to death by hanging. However, the prisoner pried loose a log from the primitive jail and escaped to Wisconsin, where he lived out a full and lawful life.

🏃 Wayside Exhibit 29: "My Old Friend Abe Lincoln"
This exhibit explores the friendship of Lincoln and Benjamin F. Harris.

*Return on IL 47 across I-74 to US 150. Turn **left** (east) on US 150 and proceed 1.3 miles, across the Sangamon River, to the next Wayside Exhibit.*

🏃 Wayside Exhibit 30: "Lincoln's Mahomet"
You'll find this exhibit on the south side of the highway on a slight rise at the New Life School. This road was part of the Fort Clark Road from Danville to Bloomington to Peoria. The ford across the Sangamon was known as Bryan's Ford, and it can still be seen under the old trestle on the north side of the road, which is now part of a scenic bike trail. Proceed a little farther to the Wayside Exhibit.

The Village of Middletown was settled on the west bank in 1836, and it was so named because it lay halfway between Danville and Bloomington. The name of the town was changed to Mahomet to avoid confusion with another Middletown in Logan County. The Bryans' home was on the east side of the ford, and it became known as the Ohio or Nine-Gal Tavern under the proprietorship of Thomas Davidson. It was so named because Davidson is said to have had nine red-headed daughters. Lincoln stayed at the inn on occasion between 1853 and 1856.

*Proceed east on US 150 into Champaign to Prospect Avenue. Turn **right** and proceed south on Prospect to University Avenue. Turn **left** (east) on University.*

CITY OF CHAMPAIGN

In 1854 the Illinois Central Railroad constructed an eastern branch that passed two miles west of Urbana. The topography north of Urbana and its small population made it impractical to lay tracks through Urbana. This decision led to the creation of the City of Champaign. The original depot was placed where University Avenue intersects with the tracks today in downtown Champaign. A town sprung up around the depot, first known as Depot City, then West Urbana, then Champaign City, and finally Champaign. The railroad spurred substantial growth in the county, but it was all in the vicinity of the depot. By 1858 the new town was larger than Urbana.

*Take University east to Randolph Street. Turn **left** (north) on Randolph and proceed to Church Street.*

The northeast corner of Church and Randolph is where wealthy entrepreneur Mark Carley, a client of Lincoln's, built his home, the first house in West Urbana. Lincoln visited here on occasion.

Continue one block north to Hill Street.

At the northwest corner of Hill and Randolph is the home of John W. Baddeley, whose early encounter with Lincoln is described in Wayside Exhibit 11 on p. 34. Some 20 years after that encounter, the now-wealthy Baddeley, living in West Urbana, frequently entertained visiting lawyers and politicians, including Lincoln. Lincoln stayed at Baddeley's home on the night of September 23, 1858, during a Senate campaign appearance in Champaign-Urbana.

*Turn **right** (east) on Hill Street and proceed to Neil Street. Turn **right** (south) on Neil, preparing to turn **left** on Main Street. Turn **left** (on Main) and drive one block to the intersection of Walnut Street and Main.*

The *Central Illinois Gazette*, predecessor of today's *News Gazette*, formerly occupied the site on the northeast corner. Its publisher was John W. Scroggs, and his editor, W. O. Stoddard, badgered Lincoln into appointing him as his third secretary during his presidency. Lincoln visited the offices here in April 1859. On December 21, 1859, the *Gazette* endorsed Lincoln for president, one of the first papers to do so.

Continue east to the intersection of Market and Main Streets.

The southeast corner of this intersection is the location of the building that housed Henry Clay Whitney's office. He arrived in 1853 and moved to Chicago in 1857. In that brief time, he became surprisingly close to Lincoln. In 1882 he published *Life on the Circuit with Lincoln*, the most complete story of Lincoln on the Circuit by a contemporary.

*Drive east and turn **right** (south) to University. Take the near (immediate) **left** under the tracks to First Street. Turn **left** immediately into the parking lot.*

Wayside Exhibit 31:
"Champaign's Lincoln"
This exhibit briefly summarizes Lincoln's time in Champaign.

*Return to University. Turn **left** (east), and proceed to Lincoln Avenue. Prepare to turn **right**.*

CITY OF URBANA

Henry Clay Whitney, West Urbana's first attorney, was a close associate of Lincoln's in both law and politics.

Urbana is the only seat Champaign County has ever had. Isaac Busey and William and Thomson R. Webber donated the land to place the new town at this location. The talented people drawn to the small city made it a welcome place for Lincoln to visit. Lincoln attended almost every court session from inclusion of the county into the Circuit in 1841 until he made his final appearance there in October 1859.

*Turn **right** and proceed south on Lincoln Avenue, across Illinois Street to the Alice Campbell Alumni Center of the University of Illinois.*

Here sits Lincoln prepared to greet returning alumni. The statue by sculptor Mark Lundeen is a gift from Gail Kelly.

*Return to Illinois Street and proceed **right** (east) to 404 W. Illinois Street.*

This house is a portion of Urbana mayor Ezekiel Boyden's home. Whitney recalled attending a tea here with Lincoln while the latter was making his Circuit rounds. Lincoln also spent the night with Boyden on September 24, 1858. Around 1919 the house was moved here from 303 W. Elm. A west wing did not survive the move, but additional space has been added to the back of the house.

*To reach the original location of Boyden House, take an immediate **left** (north) on Birch Street and proceed to Elm Street. Turn **right** (east) and proceed to 303 Elm Street, now an empty lot, near the southwest corner of Elm and Cedar.*

♟ This is the original location of the Boyden House.

*Continue east on Elm Street to Race Street. Turn **right** on Race Street and proceed south through the **right-left** jog on Washington, then back on Race Street to Carle Park (across the street from Urbana High School). Stop at the statue of Abraham Lincoln.*

♟ In addition to practicing law, Joseph Cunningham purchased and published the *Urbana Union*, converting its politics to an antislavery agenda. Another early Circuit lawyer who became wealthy by investing in real estate, Cunningham wrote a reliable county history published in 1905. In 1914 he gave a talk to the Alliance Chapter of the Daughters of the American Revolution, resulting in the formation of the organization that created the system of County Line and Courthouse Circuit Markers.

Joseph Cunningham, who came to Urbana in 1853, was the last surviving lawyer who rode the Circuit with Lincoln.

Young Lawyer, *by Lorado Taft, commissioned by Joseph Cunningham, originally stood in front of the Urbana Lincoln Hotel in 1927. It was moved to Carle Park in 1932. A plaster copy of this statue stands on the Lincoln College campus in Lincoln, Illinois, and a small replica is in the Lincoln Tomb.*

The Alschuler photograph.

Turn around and proceed north on Race Street to the southwest corner of Race and Main Streets.

Wayside Exhibit 32: "Lincoln and Photography"

Lincoln has a hint of a smile in this photograph. It was taken by Samuel Alschuler on April 25, 1858, while Lincoln attended the spring court session in Urbana. Lincoln arrived for the sitting in a white suit, which Alschuler thought would not photograph well. The short, squat Alschuler convinced the much taller Lincoln to wear the photographer's coat, which fit at the shoulders but

The American House Hotel, where Lincoln frequently stayed, was on the north side of the block between Race Street and the courthouse.

the sleeves barely reached Lincoln's elbows. This caused Lincoln's restrained smile.

Alschuler's studio was on the second floor of the Lowenstein Building, which was on the northeast corner of Main and Race.

*Turn **right** on Main and proceed east toward the courthouse.*

The proprietor of the American House announced meals by striking a loud gong, much to the annoyance of the attorneys. Lincoln retaliated by hiding the offending object, until the innkeeper's anger with its disappearance increased enough that he quietly returned it.

Continue east to the courthouse.

A Courthouse Marker appears toward the east end of the south side of the Urbana Courthouse.

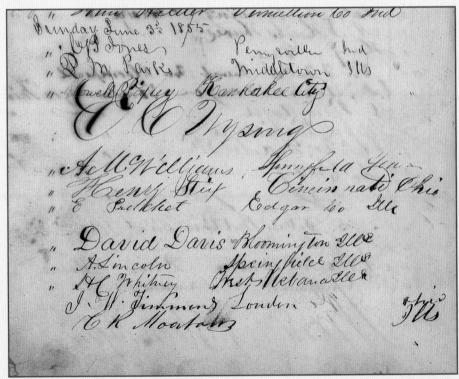

The registry of the American House Hotel includes signatures of David Davis, Lincoln, and other Circuit lawyers.

Wayside Exhibit 33: "Urbana's Lincoln"

The original courthouse square, initially divided by Walnut Street, occupied the west half of the existing courthouse site. The original log courthouse was replaced by a frame building, which was replaced with the construction of the 1848 courthouse. Lincoln tried many cases here and frequently sat as a substitute judge when David Davis was absent. The frame building was moved across Walnut to the southeast corner of what was then the intersection of Main and Walnut. It was converted to an inn called the Pennsylvania House, where Lincoln also stayed on occasion.

Lincoln ran a footrace down this block of Main Street against Samuel Waters, the proprietor of the Pennsylvania House, on May 12, 1851. An observer succinctly stated that "Abe beat." The streets that approach the courthouse site demonstrate the small size of the original platted town of Urbana. Main Street is connected to two roads that travel west: the original Main Street, once the Danville to Bloomington Road, and Springfield Avenue, part of the Terre Haute–Springfield Road. Main Street meanders as it comes from the east, following the path of that original road. The immediate area of the courthouse consists of conventional east-west, north-south streets with the blocks that were part of the original plat.

Champaign County Courthouse, constructed by Decatur's Edward O. Smith in 1848, as it looked in the 1850s. This picture shows an extensively remodeled courthouse, done some ten years later in part to prevent the move of the county seat to the booming Champaign City.

*Proceed east on Main Street, across Vine Street to Grove Street, then turn **right** (south) and proceed to Green Street. Turn **left** (east) on Green and proceed to Cottage Grove. Turn **right** (south) on Cottage Grove and proceed to Philo Road. Angle **left** (east) on Philo Road to Washington Street, turn **left** (east) and proceed out of Urbana. Continue east to a T intersection (C 1800 E); turn **right** (south) and drive 0.2 miles to C 1525 N. Turn **left** and proceed east 4.3 miles across Salt Fork to the next Wayside Exhibit.*

Kelley's Tavern, built in the early 1830s, was a popular stop between Urbana and Danville.

🏃 Wayside Exhibit 34: "Kelley's Tavern"
Kelley's Tavern was operated by Joseph Kelley from 1849 to 1864. The town of St. Joseph is named for him. Whitney recalls first meeting Lincoln, Davis, and Swett, whom he called the "great triumvirate" of the Circuit, at Kelley's on June 3, 1854.

🎩 Salt Fork is one of several branches of the Vermilion River that the Circuit riders crossed. The first bridge across this fork was built in 1837, but it was swept away within a year. Travelers crossed the river by ford or ferry depending on the season.

Continue east approximately 3.6 miles, cross the inlet of Homer Lake, and arrive at a small park on the south side of the road.

🏃 Wayside Exhibit 35: "On the Bloomington Road: The Clark Neighborhood"
This exhibit tells the story of the historic road between Danville and Bloomington and the nearby settlement it spawned.

Continue 2.3 miles east to the next County Line Marker, at C 2800 E.

9 Champaign-Vermilion: The Marker is on the north side of the road (GPS: N 40°04'31.8", W 87°56'20.9").

This monument was generously repaired by an unknown person, whose work is clearly visible.

Note your mileage at this point and watch for a granite courthouse-style Marker 2.4 miles from the county line.

VERMILION (DANVILLE)

VERMILION COUNTY, SETTLED IN 1819 AND LEGALLY FORMED

in 1826, was one of the largest and most influential counties in the Circuit. Key residents supported Lincoln politically, and he found a significant source of legal business there. The State of Illinois was settled from the south, moving north along the Mississippi River on the west and the Indiana line on the east. Settlements to the interior of the state lagged behind. Danville and Paris on the eastern edge of Illinois developed earlier than the county seats to the west.

Continue east on the gravel road.

This road, known as the Lincoln Trail Road, which has never been paved, is one of the most authentic stretches that Lincoln followed. The terrain from here to Danville is the roughest but also the most scenic of the Circuit. The road passes the Bodkin Cemetery; its early dates on the gravestones tell us that the cemetery was there as Lincoln rode past.

An odd courthouse-style Marker appears 2.4 miles from the county line. It marks the farm of John R. Thompson, who was not a contemporary of

A thunderstorm threatens on the Lincoln Trail Road.

As the road descends toward the picturesque crossing at Stony Creek, numerous "witness oaks" stand, which saw the semiannual passage by Lincoln and his fellow lawyers.

Lincoln's. It is not known why Lottie Jones, the driving force behind the Lincoln Circuit Marker project, placed one of the granite courthouse-style Markers at this site.

Judge Davis reported in a letter to his wife in May 1852 that rain caused him, Lincoln, and State's Attorney David Campbell to spend the night here at "the Smith farm . . . a beautiful place."

Continue east across the intersection with 500 E.
*Follow the Lincoln Circuit road across Stony Creek, then along a ridge to a T intersection, C 700 E (the Lincoln Circuit road probably went straight); turn **left** and proceed to US 150, then **right** (east) and proceed on US 150 toward Oakwood, running parallel to the Lincoln road.*

After the turn onto US 150, look at the large home on the south side of the road. Willis Hubbard lived in an earlier house on this site, and Lincoln occasionally stayed there.

Proceed east on US 150. This road runs parallel to, but is slightly north of, the path of the Lincoln Circuit road.

Immediately before descending to cross the Middle Fork of the Vermilion River, you'll see the entrance to the Sportsman Club on the right. This private property includes the actual location of the sharply sloping road the lawyers took to the river crossing.

Proceed down the hill on US 150 and across the Middle Fork of the Vermilion River.

The Vermilion is the site of the Salines, a highly profitable commercial salt operation, which was the first settlement in the county in 1819. It was operated a few years after its startup by John Vance, a client and political ally of Lincoln's. Vance was instrumental in the formation of Champaign County.

*Take the first **right** after crossing the river (Batestown Road). Proceed up the hill 0.7 miles and turn at the first **right**, Shangri La Road.*

This is Kistler Hill, perhaps the most demanding section of road on the Circuit. Today's road descends steeply toward the river before taking an abrupt left halfway down the hill. The original road used by Lincoln probably continued straight here to the ford of the Middle Fork. Descending this hill gives you a sense of the steep climb the travelers had to make.

*Proceed across the river. Turn around there, and return on Shangri La. At the end of Shangri La, turn **right** and drive east to US 150, where the road becomes four lanes. Then proceed east on US 150 to the bridge across the North Fork of the Vermilion River.*

As you approach and cross the North Fork, look for three points of interest.

The first is the Lincoln Circuit road here, a path north of US 150 running parallel to the North Fork of the Vermilion.

The second is a footbridge in Ellsworth Park that spans the North Fork parallel to the highway bridge and marks where the lawyers crossed.

The third is a Courthouse Marker at the east end of the bridge on the north side of the road. This Marker is located here rather than the usual location at the courthouse site.

*After crossing the bridge, turn immediately **right** and descend to the entrance of the park. Enter the park and drive to the footbridge.*

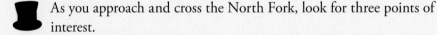

The bluff on the east side of the river was too steep for the riders to ascend as they approached Danville. They rode south, almost to the river's junction, and ascended the hill there to Main Street, on the road that you are taking out of the park.

Proceed back to Main Street and enter Danville by that same route, turning right (east) on Main.

CITY OF DANVILLE

The Salines' location and terrain were not suitable for a town, so the mouth of the North Fork was chosen. The town was founded by Dan Beckwith, a surveyor who settled in 1819 to establish a fur trading outpost, and the city of Danville is named after him. Gurdon Saltonstall Hubbard followed him, creating a larger post in 1824 as part of the American Fur Company. Hubbard platted a road north to Chicago, known as the Hubbard Trace, which followed the approximate path of today's Illinois Route 1. Vermilion County became part of the Eighth Judicial Circuit in 1845, an outcome prompted by the efforts of David Davis, then a legislator, to even the political imbalance caused by the inclusion of Democratic Shelby County in the Circuit. Vermilion remained in the Eighth Circuit throughout Lincoln's career.

Walking Tour of Main Street in Danville

Continue east on Main Street 0.2 miles to the drive-in bank on the north side of Main. Park near the bank, then walk east toward the courthouse at the corner of Main and Vermilion Street.

This is the same road that the Circuit lawyers took to the McCormack House. Lincoln spent many evenings regaling his audience with countless stories in the inn's public room. Lew Wallace, author of *Ben Hur*, then a lawyer from nearby Covington, Indiana, recalled an informal joke-telling contest between Lincoln and four Indiana lawyers. One by one the Indiana attorneys dropped out as their supply of jokes was exhausted. Wallace said, "At last he [Lincoln] took the floor and held it." Henry Clay Whitney remembered Danville as one of the most congenial and enjoyable stops on the Circuit, partly because of the enjoyable time spent at the inn. Lincoln's letter, dated November 14, 1859, accepting an invitation to speak at Cooper Institute in New York the following February, was written on McCormack House stationary.

The McCormack House, opened by Jesse Gilbert in 1833, was one of the most accommodating hotels on the Circuit. It stood where the bank is now located.

In 1859 Dr. W. W. Woodbury built the tallest structure in Danville on the south side of Main Street. He named it Lincoln Hall, causing the humble Lincoln a certain amount of embarrassment.

Wayside Exhibit 36:
"Danville's Lincoln"

Lincoln's personal and professional growth over the years while visiting Danville is detailed on the exhibit in front of the Danville City Hall on the south side of Main. It describes the McCormack House, his friendship with Ward Hill Lamon, and his close relationship with Oscar and Elizabeth Harmon.

W. W. Woodbury, a Lincoln supporter, owned a drug and general goods store where Lincoln frequently purchased medicine, books, stationary, and other supplies. The Woodbury Store stood near Lincoln Hall at the southwest corner of the public square.

This photograph of Lincoln, done by Amon T. Joslin, was taken on or about May 27, 1857, while Lincoln was in Danville for the Circuit court session.

Amon T. Joslin's photography gallery was on the second floor of the building adjoining the Woodbury Drug Store.

The Lincoln-era courthouse, 50 by 50 feet and designed in the coffee mill style, was built by Gurdon Hubbard in 1832 and located at the same location as the current courthouse.

This panorama shows the area of the Vermilion County Courthouse in the Lincoln era.

Lincoln and Ward Hill Lamon had an office on the second floor of the Barnum Building, which was located on the site of the existing building known as the "skyscraper" west of the courthouse. While Lincoln held forth at the McCormack House several doors to the west, Lamon would round up a few hard drinkers and return to the office for some serious consumption of alcohol.

Continue walking on the west side of Vermilion to the northeast corner of Presky Park.

Wayside Exhibit 37: "Lincoln's Danville Friends"
Lincoln had many friends in Danville, including Oliver Davis, Enoch Kingsbury, Dr. W. W. Woodbury, and Oscar and Elizabeth Harmon. A period map of the city shows the location of the home of each "friend."

Ward Hill Lamon.

This ends your walking tour.

Return to your vehicle and drive east past the courthouse to the home of Oscar and Elizabeth Harmon at 522 E. Main Street.

🎩 The Harmons lived in this brick house on a 30-acre tract. Lincoln occasionally stayed here while attending court, including one Thanksgiving.

Proceed back west on Main Street to the Depot of the Great Western Railroad at the northeast corner of the intersection of Main and the tracks.

🎩 Lincoln frequently traveled on the Great Western to and from this depot for law-related, as well as political, visits.

This was Lincoln's last stop in Illinois on February 11, 1861, as his

Oscar Harmon, a brilliant lawyer and supporter of Lincoln, who partnered with Oliver Davis. He raised a regiment of volunteers and led them through many battles before he was killed in action in January 1864 at Kennesaw Mountain, Georgia.

AI RAM LINCOLN,
Springfield.

W. H. LAMON,
Danville.

Lincoln & Lamon,
ATTORNYS AT LAW,

HAVING formed a co-partnership, will practice in the Courts of the Eighth Judicial Circuit, and the Superior Court, and all business entrusted to hem will be attended to with promptness and fidelity ☞ *Office on the second floor of the Barnum blding over Whitcomb's Store.*

Lincoln and Lamon formed a loose arrangement to share law business in Vermilion County, as evidenced by this Danville newspaper ad. The arrangement generated a substantial amount of business for Lincoln in the county.

Elizabeth Harmon, Oscar's beautiful wife, who had an exceptional rapport with Lincoln.

Washington-bound train came through from Springfield. About 1,000 people, including Elizabeth Harmon, William Fithian, and Oliver Davis, witnessed his final appearance in the state as he spoke from the back of the train in a steady drizzle.

*Proceed west to the courthouse, turn **right** (north) onto Vermilion, then proceed one block and turn **left** (west) on North Street to the corner of North and Franklin Streets.*

Oliver Davis, to whom Lincoln referred to as "Little Davis," was Danville's best lawyer of the era. He associated with Lincoln frequently and also opposed him on many cases.

Lincoln and Judge Davis occasionally attended the First Presbyterian Church at this location while in Danville for the court sessions.

Danville Depot.

Proceed west to Pine Street. Turn **left** *on Pine and turn into the VFW parking lot. This was the site of the Red Seminary.*

Enoch Kingsbury, the Presbyterian minister who arrived in 1831, was an ardent opponent of slavery. Lincoln liked him well enough to appoint him as the local postmaster.

The Red Seminary, operated by the Danville Methodist Church, was located where the VFW parking lot is today. It was the subject of a bitter rivalry for community preeminence with the competing seminary of the Presbyterian Church, which erupted into a heated libel suit between Methodist George Casseday and Presbyterian William Fithian, who Lincoln represented. Casseday attacked Fithian's character relentlessly in the local newspapers, tagging him with such derogatory titles such as "human monster" and "unfeeling reptile." The high-profile case resulted in a verdict in Fithian's favor in the amount of $547.90, which Casseday later inventoried in his personal property tax return as "the character of Dr. Fithian—$547.90."

One night, while in town for the court session, Lincoln disappeared from the usual festivities at the McCormack House and walked up to the seminary to view what David Davis called a "magic light show," which so enthralled him that he returned the next night.

Return to North Street and continue west to Gilbert Street. Turn **right** *(north) on Gilbert and go one block. Turn* **left** *on Lafayette Street and proceed to 116 Gilbert Street, the home of Dr. William Fithian, with the Vermilion County Museum behind it.*

Fithian, a hard-working doctor, made a fortune in land west of town. He first engaged Lincoln as a lawyer and brought him to Danville in 1841; Lincoln represented him on a number of cases over the years. Fithian, a powerful Whig legislator who steadfastly promoted Lincoln, was one of

William Fithian, a doctor and influential politician, was an early booster of Lincoln, both professionally and politically.

several people around the Circuit whose support was strategically essential to Lincoln's professional and political rise. Lincoln's room in the southwest corner of the house is maintained as it was when he stayed here on September 21, 1858. As Lincoln rode in Fithian's carriage from the depot, a long procession followed. After dinner at Fithian's home, the crowd was still clamoring for Lincoln to speak, so he stepped through the bedroom window onto the existing balcony in his stocking feet to briefly address the enthusiastic gathering.

Wayside Exhibit 38: "A Friend Forever"

This exhibit details Lincoln's strong friendship with Fithian.

The Vermilion County History Museum, includes both Fithian's home and an enlarged replica of the Lincoln-era courthouse. The first floor of the "courthouse" includes a statue of Lincoln by Rick Harney. The second floor has an informative exhibit including a re-creation of the Lamon-Lincoln law office that contains some of its actual furniture.

The next stop on the Circuit was Paris, so the lawyers headed south on the Vincennes Trace, which is now IL Route 1 and US 150.

Return to Gilbert Street and drive south on Gilbert across the bridge.

The street was named for Jesse Gilbert, proprietor of the McCormack House, who also ran a ferry used by travelers to cross the Vermilion here.

Proceed south out of Danville on IL 1, through Tilton, Westville, Georgetown, and Olivet to Ridge Farm. Enter Ridge Farm and proceed south 0.7 miles to 204 S. State Street, opposite an intersecting street, East Ridge.

The town of Ridge Farm grew around the farm of the same name, an enterprise of Abraham Smith, a Quaker and the town's first postmaster.

The traveling lawyers occasionally stayed at his home, which is still standing at 204 N. State Street. Smith was an abolitionist and temperance zealot who thought little of Lincoln and so informed him. In 1853 his remarks about the drinking problem of State's Attorney David Campbell provoked Campbell to sue Smith for slander, which resulted in a $600 verdict against Smith. Lincoln represented Campbell while Oliver Davis defended Smith. Some five years later, Smith was so moved by the "House Divided Speech" that he reversed his opinion of Lincoln.

Drive south to the County Line and stop.

10 Vermilion-Edgar: You'll find the County Line Marker at the southeast corner of IL 1 and C 100 N (GPS: W 39°52'49.4", W 87°39'17.9").

EDGAR (PARIS)

EDGAR WAS ONE OF THREE COUNTIES OF THE CIRCUIT TO

which European settlers had arrived by the time of statehood in 1818, the others being Shelby and Sangamon. In 1850 it was the fourth largest county in the Circuit. Lincoln regularly practiced law there from 1845 to 1853, but he terminated his practice there when it was removed from the Circuit. This reduction as part of the reduction of the Circuit from 14 to 8 counties was pursuant to a bill shepherded through the legislature by Lincoln acting as lobbyist, at the request of Judge Davis. Politically, it was difficult for him to gain much traction because many pro-slavery inhabitants relocated here from the south. Lincoln carried the county in 1858, but lost it in 1860 and 1864.

As you drive south, note the network of creeks the lawyers had to traverse on the way to Paris: Crabapple Creek, the north and south forks of Brouillette Creek, Snake Creek, and Sugar Creek, Paris's present water source. In an 1840 letter to his wife Sarah, David Davis described the trip from Danville to Paris: "The Country the whole distance is beautiful to the eye—much better improved than in McLean and Tazewell."

IL 1 is the former historic Vincennes Trace, which Lincoln traveled from Danville to Paris. Lincoln passed the Trace's mile Markers as he headed south.

The road passes through Bloomfield where Lincoln sometimes stayed at the Alexander Somerville Hotel, *which was located at the southwest corner of IL 1 and C 1050 N.* Lincoln advocated temperance here during the 1830s, although there is no record of the content of the speech.

Continue south on IL 1. Note the mileage at the intersection of IL 1 and US 36. As you proceed south you'll see two surviving Vincennes Trace mile Markers located on the east side of the road. The first is 1.6 miles south of US 36. The site of the second one is 4 miles further (5.6 miles south of the intersection). The second one stood at the intersection of IL 1 and C 1625 N. This Marker itself was recently destroyed, but the protective concrete still stands. The markers are identical, and this is the safer of the two places to stop.

CITY OF PARIS

Samuel Vance donated 26 acres to Edgar County for the location of its county seat, with the condition that it be named Paris. The city was a cultural outpost in the early pioneer days of middle Illinois, boasting a Presbyterian Church founded in 1824, the Paris Academy founded in the early 1830s, and a newspaper started in 1836, which was replaced shortly thereafter by the influential *Prairie Beacon.* Its proximity to Terre Haute across the Wabash River brought lawyers from Indiana to the county's courts, including John P. Usher, who would serve President Lincoln as secretary of the interior.

Follow the highway into Paris to Central Avenue and to the northwest corner of the courthouse lawn.

 Note the Courthouse Marker at this corner.

Kirby Benedict was a strong Democrat who was appointed by Franklin Pierce in 1852 to the Supreme Court of the Territory of New Mexico. With the support of David Davis, Lincoln reappointed Benedict in 1862. Lincoln's respect for Benedict's legal ability overcame objections to his appointment because of alcohol abuse. Tragically, Benedict died a hopeless alcoholic in 1874 in Santa Fe, New Mexico.

*Proceed all the way around the courthouse square and leave the square to the west on Wood Street. Proceed west to Sheriff and Wood Streets, turn **left** (south) on Sheriff, and stop.*

This coffee-mill style courthouse, built in 1832 by Leander Munsell of Paris, served the county until 1891. Munsell built similar courthouses in Charleston, Bloomington, and Decatur.

🎩 Leander Munsell's home was on the right side of Sheriff Street.

*Turn **left** and drive south on Sheriff to Court Street and stop.*

🎩 The park east of the Methodist church, across Court Street, is the site of the home of William P. Dole, a solid Lincoln supporter who had moved to Paris from Terre Haute. Lincoln appointed Dole as commissioner of Indian affairs, a post he held throughout the entire Lincoln presidency. One of Lincoln's last communications was to Dole on April 14, 1865: "Do not send off the commission . . . until . . . hearing from me again."

Kirby Benedict, first of Decatur, then of Paris, was one of the best trial lawyers on the Circuit. He argued many cases with and against Lincoln in both venues.

The courthouse square appears much the same as it did in Lincoln's time. The photo shows a "Campaign Pole," a contrivance used by both parties in the mid-nineteenth century. These immense wooden poles were raised by competing political partisans to support their respective candidates. This pole was raised in the 1870s.

 There is an excellent "Looking for Lincoln" display in a store front at 118 W. Court. It thoroughly describes the Lincoln sites in Paris.

*Turn **left** (east) on Court Street.*
Proceed past the courthouse square, across Main, to the southeast corner of Main and Court.
Proceed east one-half block to 116–18 E. Court Street, then stop.

The Green Tree Hotel was a welcome successor to earlier Paris taverns, one of which David Davis characterized as "about the meanest tavern you ever saw." Lincoln and his fellow lawyers frequently visited the Green Tree, the back door of which opened into Alexander Grove, a stand of hardwoods owned by Washington Alexander that was often used for public events.

This photo, taken in 1878, shows the north side of Court Street, east of Main, along which Lincoln walked to the Green Tree Hotel.

The Green Tree Hotel, which stood on this site, opened in the early 1850s and was one of the more gracious inns on the Circuit.

*Turn **right** (south) in the alley between the two buildings, and proceed*
through the block that takes you onto Washington Street at a point that
would have once been in the center of Alexander Grove.

*Turn **right** (west) on Washington Street and drive to Central. Stop*
at the Milton K. Alexander House at the southeast corner of Central
and Washington.

Wayside Exhibit 39: "Lincoln and Milton K. Alexander"

This exhibit tells of the relationship between Lincoln and Milton K. Alexander, the county's leading Democrat, who was a client of Lincoln's but who also was opposed by Lincoln in some cases. The exhibit also guides you to other Lincoln points of interest: the Carnegie Library at 207 S. Main and the Edgar County Historical Society Annex at 408 N. main.

Milton Alexander opened the first store in Paris in 1823 and was the postmaster for 32 years. His house was the first brick building in Edgar County, before twelve of the other Circuit counties had even been created. It was built in 1828, indicative of the early development of Paris. Both Lincoln and Douglas visited this home.

*Go **left** on Central Avenue and proceed to US 150/IL 16. (Note your mileage*
*at this intersection.) Turn **right** and proceed west on IL 16 for 7.5 miles to*
*Anglin Road (C 750 E). Turn **left** (southwest) on Anglin Road and proceed*
into Grandview. This is clearly the old Circuit road. Stop at the T intersec-
*tion in Grandview (C 625 E). Turn **left** and stop at the intersection with*
C 510 N.

TOWN OF GRANDVIEW

Visiting tiny Grandview is like stepping back into the nineteenth century. A portion of the building at the southeast corner of this intersection on a small knoll used to be the Barnett Hotel, where Lincoln and Circuit lawyers stayed on occasion. The rough-hewn timbers of the frame of this house confirm its history.

Proceed south past the town hall, which has been at this location since 1831.
*Stop at the intersection with C 500 N. Go **right** (west) 0.3 miles to the third*

right turn, known as Stage Coach Road (C 490 N). This is the actual road taken between Grandview and points west by Lincoln and his contemporaries. Proceed west to C 125 E where the Stage Coach Road surface becomes gravel, as it has never been paved. Continue west 1.3 miles to the next County Line Marker.

Edgar-Coles: The County Line Marker is on the north side of the road (GPS: N 39°30'34", W 87°57'42.1").

4. HEADING WEST AND THEN HOME

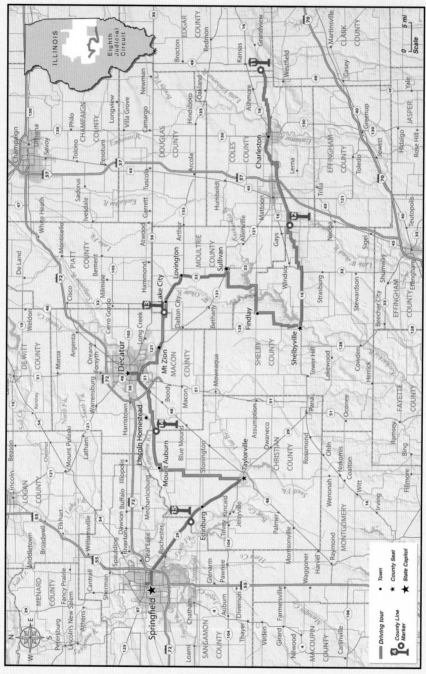

Map showing the south central part of the Circuit.

COLES (CHARLESTON)

COLES COUNTY WAS NEVER PART OF THE CIRCUIT, ALTHOUGH

it is bordered on three sides by Circuit counties, and the lawyers had to travel through Coles as they made their way from Edgar to Shelby.

> *Proceed west from the County Line Marker across IL 49 on C 850 N. Go 0.1 miles and veer **right** (west) at the fork. Continue west at the intersection with C 2600 E, past the gas storage facility, past C 2420 E, C 2400 E, and C 2360 E, to a T intersection, C 2270 E. Turn **left** (south) on C 2270 E and go to C 850 N, turn **right** (west) and proceed to C 2150 E. Turn **left** (south) and proceed to C 830 N (Arrowhead Road). Turn **right** (west) and proceed 2.4 miles to Harrison Street Road (C 770 N). Turn **right** (west) onto Harrison, cross the Embarras (pronounced "EM-braw") River, and proceed to IL 16. Cross IL 16 in a northerly direction and follow that road, which becomes Harrison Avenue. Proceed west on Harrison to 7th Street. Turn **right** (north) to the courthouse square. Park on the square.*

CITY OF CHARLESTON

Charleston is the county seat of Coles. Lincoln had a substantial volume of business here, and he made close acquaintances both professionally and personally with Charleston attorneys.

The plaque from the Courthouse Marker had originally been placed in the usual granite monument, but at some point the block was removed and the plaque now hangs on the south side of the county courthouse.

Lincoln engaged with several lawyers in Charleston, including Usher F. Linder and Orlando Ficklin, both of whom were political opponents. Lincoln's famous and somewhat curious case *In Re Bryant*, commonly known as the Matson Slave Case, was tried in Charleston. Lincoln's involvement in

Coles County Courthouse in the Lincoln era.

the case has raised questions in the minds of Lincoln scholars for years, as well as various theories as to why he participated in it. Hiram Rutherford, a doctor and abolitionist from Oakland, Illinois, hired Ficklin to free slaves Jane Bryant and her four children. Their owner, Robert Matson, had brought them from his plantation in Kentucky to work the cornfields. Their presence in Illinois for over a year freed them under state law. Matson wanted to return his property back to Kentucky, but Ficklin sought a writ of habeas corpus to prevent this. Matson hired Usher Linder, who engaged Lincoln to help the slave owner prevail. The efforts of Linder and Lincoln were unsuccessful, and the slaves were freed.

> *Drive north, leaving the Courthouse square, and continue to Madison Avenue. Turn **left** (west), then bear **right** on State Street and proceed to E Street (C 1550 E), which is the Fairgrounds. Turn **left** and go to the statue depicting Lincoln and Douglas in front of the Debate Museum.*
>
> *Continue south to Madison. Turn **right** and drive west past the Fairgrounds, around a sharp corner; the road immediately intersects with Old State Road (C 850 N). Turn **left** (west) and follow it as it winds southwest, crossing Riley Creek, to IL 16.*

Lincoln-era travelers actually took this road out of Charleston to travel west. On maps of the period, the road can be seen crossing today's IL 16 through the present airport and continuing on the other side of the airport.

This is Robert Root's painting of the Lincoln-Douglas Debate in Charleston on September 18, 1858. It is included to show the images of three Circuit lawyers: (1) Orlando Ficklin, (2) Usher Linder, and (3) Richard J. Oglesby. Discussion of this debate is beyond the focus of this book.

*Turn **right** (west) on IL 16, stay in the **left** lane and go 0.6 miles to Loxa Road (C 1050 E). Follow it around the airport to C 650 N (Lancer Road). Proceed **right** and follow the road west to a T intersection (C 1105 E), then go north until it turns **left** (west) again at C 680 N (this resumes the Old State Road). Proceed west across Lerna Road (C 870 E), continue west over I 57, then continue farther west across C 280 E (Lakeland Boulevard), and continue west on Old State Road (C 280 E) for 4.2 miles to C 100 E. Stop.*

12 **A.** Coles-Shelby: Stop at the southeast corner of the intersection of C 450 N and C 100 E. The plaque in the brick wall here (GPS: N 39°26'37.4", W 88°26'59.2") was relocated from the original County Line Marker, which was destroyed at its original location. This is not the Shelby County Line.

Proceed west 0.9 miles to the county line at the intersection of C 1555 N and C 3600 E (so designated by Shelby County); C 450 N (also labeled Old State Road), and C 1000 E (so designated by Coles County). Each of the different roads is marked by each county using different call numbers.

12 **B.** Coles-Shelby: This T intersection marks the actual county line. On the south side of the road you can see the base of the Marker from which the plaque was taken (GPS: N 39°26'23.5", W 88°28'00.9"). The county name plates are still on the base.

SHELBY (SHELBYVILLE)

Shelby County was one of the oldest in the Circuit, first settled in 1818 and formally created in 1827. It was part of the Circuit from 1841 to 1845, and then again from 1847 to 1853. Much of its population hailed from Kentucky and Tennessee; accordingly, it was heavily Democratic and pro-slavery. The county never supported Lincoln politically, and he essentially quit practicing law there when it was removed from the Circuit. He made no political appearances in Shelby County after the 1856 election.

SIDE TRIP. Go to the Oakland, Illinois, home and office of Hiram Rutherford; you may want to call ahead as they are not always open. Although these sites are off the Circuit route, the importance of the Matson Slave Case and its locale justify inclusion here. Unfortunately, Oakland is about a 20-mile round trip to the north. About one mile west of the Shelby-Coles county

Black Horse Tavern, a frequent stop on the Circuit, was operated by the Tressler family. David Davis wrote in a letter to Sarah, "The old lady keeps an excellent house." Martin Van Buren stayed at this tavern during his post-presidency tour of the West.

line, you will intersect with IL 49. Turn right (north). Consult a map to determine the balance of the directions. If you pursue the trip, return here to resume the Circuit travel.

> *Drive west around a sharp **left** turn (south) to C 1500 N. Turn **right** (west) and proceed to C 3400 E. Turn **left** (south) to C 1450 N, then turn **right** (west) to C 3200 E. Turn **left** (south) on C 3200 E, and proceed around a curve to the west (C 1425 N), then continue west to the intersection of C 1425 N and C 3050 E.*
>
> *Proceed west from Black Horse Tavern on C 1425 N (a dirt road) to C 3000 E, a T intersection. Turn **left** on C 3000 E and drive south to C 1400 N. Go **right** (west) on C 1400 N to C 2900 E, a T intersection. Turn **right** (north) and drive to C 1300 N (IL 16). Turn **left** and proceed west into Shelbyville, crossing the Kaskaskia River, called "the Okaw" in this stretch.*

Shelbyville sits on Brewster's Bluff above the Okaw. The bluff was too steep to climb by horse, so travelers had to cross at a downstream ford at the back of an existing campground a few hundred yards downstream. You can still observe the point of exit from the river on the west side. To reach the town, the old road continued from that ford up the bluff, where you can still see traces of the road. The ford and the old road are on private property.

TOWN OF SHELBYVILLE

Take IL 16 across the river to the courthouse square and park the car.

Walking Tour of Downtown Shelbyville

Begin the tour in front of the courthouse.

The current courthouse is the third, dedicated in 1883. The Lincoln-era courthouse stood in the middle of the square, now known as Lincoln Square, where three monuments have been set. The first is a boulder at the southeast corner marking the site of the original courthouse. The second is the Civil War monument designed by Root. The third is the Courthouse Marker at the northwest corner.

The John McClarey statue depicts Lincoln and prominent Shelbyville lawyer Anthony Thornton debating the issues of the presidential race of 1856.

This Robert Root painting depicts Shelbyville's courthouse square in Lincoln's time. It shows the courthouse and, to the right, the Tackett House, also called the Talman House, where the lawyers stayed. The tourism office is now at the site of the Tackett House.

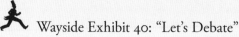 Wayside Exhibit 40: "Let's Debate"

The Lincoln-Thornton Debate took place on August 9, 1856, during the Frémont-Buchanan presidential campaign. Lincoln spoke at great length and received rebuttals from both Thornton and Shelbyville attorney Samuel Moulton. Robert Root's painting of the debate hangs in the Circuit courtroom, with a chart identifying those Shelbyville citizens depicted in the painting.

When you enter the courthouse, inquire at the Circuit clerk's office whether it is appropriate to enter the courtroom. Portraits of Thornton and Moulton, both of whom participated in the 1883 dedication of the courthouse, hang on the east wall of the courtroom.

Return to the street and walk to the east side of the parking lot of the Tourism Center.

Robert Root's painting of the Lincoln-Thornton Debate. In addition to Lincoln: Samuel Moulton was a Democrat who was always soft on slavery but became more so as the war approached. He is seated to Lincoln's immediate right. Anthony Thornton was Lincoln's principal opponent in this event, but they remained friends. Thornton is seated in front of the table. Later in 1856, Thornton recovered a judgment on behalf of his client, Lincoln, to collect a fee that Lincoln had earned in a Moultrie County case. John Ward, an ally and friend of Lincoln's, is circled.

Wayside Exhibit 41: "Traveling the Circuit"

This exhibit tells more about Lincoln and the Circuit. It describes the camaraderie enjoyed by the lawyers. It also discusses a number of taverns, including the well-run Tackett House. You'll also learn about the treacherous travel conditions and the occasional loneliness of life on the Circuit.

Walk to the exhibit in front of the building.

 Wayside Exhibit 42: "Anthony Thornton"

The exhibit tells the story of Anthony Thornton, a Whig and Lincoln's associate, friend, and political ally-turned-opponent after the Kansas-Nebraska Act of 1854.

Enter the Tourism Center and visit with the friendly staff. Enjoy a wide variety of tourist brochures, including some related to Lincoln and Shelbyville.

 Wayside Exhibit 43: "Samuel Moulton"

The exhibit details the career of Samuel Moulton, a longtime political opponent of Lincoln's. As of this writing, the exhibit is displayed in the tourism office and has not yet been placed at its permanent site.

Taken in the late 1860s, this photograph looking east from where the visitor is standing, shows the scene much as it would have appeared in Lincoln's time. The courthouse appears to sit in the middle of today's Main Street, then a dead end because there was no road coming up the bluff.

Walk west on Main Street, on the north side of the street, to the intersection with North Broadway.

Cross Main Street to the South City Mini-Park, site of another Wayside Marker.

🏃 Wayside Exhibit 44: "Lincoln's Court Cases"

This exhibit gives an overview of Lincoln's law practice. He mostly handled debt cases, which included the defense of 17 suits brought against Shelbyville residents by the Terre Haute and Alton Railroad to collect stock subscriptions. He also argued a number of slander cases, some of which were based on marital infidelity, leading one Lincoln scholar to refer to the town as "a Peyton Place."

*Walk back to the courthouse square on the south side of the street. Turn **right** (south) on S. Washington Street and proceed two blocks to the Shelby County Historical and Genealogical Society.*

🎩 Visit the Lincoln Room's collection about Lincoln in Shelbyville. The building is the old County Jail.

This ends your walking tour.

*Return to your car, drive west on Main Street to Morgan Street. Turn **right** and drive to N. 3rd Street. Turn **right** on 3rd and go to the driveway entrance of the private home that once belonged to Anthony Thornton and stop.*

Anthony Thornton's gracious home was built in 1851. Thornton served on the Illinois Supreme Court in the 1870s and was the first president of the Illinois State Bar Association. He was succeeded as president by David Davis.

*Proceed north on Morgan to N. 12th Street. Turn **left** (west) and proceed to N. Broadway, going **right** (north) around a **right-hand** curve (C 1500 N) to C 1860 E. Turn **left** (north) and drive to 1600 N, then turn **right** (east), then **left** (north) on C 1875 E for 1.8 miles to C 1800 N; turn **right** on C 1800 N and proceed east 1.1 miles to the first farmhouse on the **left**, with a large oak in front, and stop.*

🎩 This is the former site of the John M. Ward home, highlighted in the Root painting (p. 91). On June 3, 1852, David Davis wrote his wife Sarah from Decatur that they had stopped here four days earlier while traveling from Shelbyville to Sullivan. "Lincoln, Anthony Thornton, Campbell, Moulton & myself went to Mr. John Ward's, about five miles from Shelbyville—lolled away several hours, got a fine dinner, and about 3 oclk [*sic*] started for Sullivan where we got about 6 ockl [*sic*]."

*Proceed east to C 2100 E. Turn **left** (north) and proceed into Finley to Division Street.*

🎩 Finley did not exist during the Lincoln era. The lawyers would head northwest to cross the Okaw River on the way to Sullivan. Lake Shelbyville now covers those roads, so you will have to detour.

Drive east from Finley over the bridge across the lake. As you do so, you are crossing the county line from Shelby into Moultrie County.

☒ Shelby-Moultrie: No County Line Marker was ever placed by the two feuding counties. This is the only county line between the 14 where a Marker was omitted.

MOULTRIE (SULLIVAN)

Moultrie was the last county in the Circuit to be formally organized. It was created from parts of eastern Macon and northern Shelby in 1843 because the residents of northeast Shelby wanted their own county, contrary to the wishes of the rest of the county. Moultrie's population at the outset was a mere 2,000. The northeast county residents petitioned the legislature for a referendum, which was held and defeated in 1842. In 1843 they persuaded the legislature to create the new county without a referendum.

This drawing depicts the first Moultrie County Courthouse, which was built in 1848 and destroyed by fire in 1864.

The circumstances surrounding the formation of the county and the placement of its seat left a long-standing enmity between Shelby and Moultrie.

Until a courthouse could be built in the newly chosen seat of Sullivan, court was held at various sites around the county. Moultrie was part of the Eighth Judicial Circuit from its formation until 1853. It was strongly Democratic and did not oppose slavery, but it did have a small contingent of antislavery partisans. Almost 100 years later, Moultrie County declined to participate in the Looking for Lincoln Wayside Exhibit effort.

> *Take the bridge across the lake. Note your mileage at the east end of the bridge; continue east 1.6 miles to Coal Shaft Bridge Road. Turn **left** (north) and proceed north across the Coal Shaft Bridge through Kirksville to C 1350 N. Turn **right** on C 1350 N, and proceed into Sullivan to a stop sign on Jackson Street.*

TOWN OF SULLIVAN

Before Sullivan was settled, two hunters, one of whom was named Asa Rice, came to a stream where the north edge of the timber met the prairie. Rice's companion dubbed the spot "Asa's Point." Several years later, two years after the formation of the county, the commissioners picked this spot for the county seat, although there was still no settlement there. They changed the name from Asa's Point to Sullivan and platted the town. Its boundaries were Jackson Street on the north, Hamilton Street on the west, Water Street on the south, and Worth Street on the east.

> *Proceed east on Jackson, where the road makes a sharp **left**, and continue to Hamilton. Turn **right** (south) on Hamilton and proceed to Harrison Street. Turn **left** (east) on Harrison and proceed to the courthouse square and park.*

The Courthouse Marker is located at the northeast corner of the square.

The home of James Elder, an early leader of the antislavery party in Moultrie County and a friend of Lincoln and Davis, stood at the southwest corner of the square, south of Harrison and west of Main. Davis preferred to stay at Elder's instead of at the larger Taylor Hotel, where most of the traveling lawyers stayed. In a letter to Sarah dated June 3, 1852, he reported that they dined at a tavern and that it "was so rough that I should have been in a bad humor to have stayed there." The Taylor Hotel was located at the northeast corner of Harrison and Main, diagonally opposite the Elder House.

To leave Sullivan, turn around, go north from the square to Jackson (IL 121), and proceed west on Jackson (IL 121), which joins IL 32 coming from the south. Follow IL 32 north to Lovington. Continue through Lovington on IL 32, across the West Fork of the Okaw River (note the mileage at the bridge). Continue on IL 32 toward Lake City, 3 miles from the bridge. Immediately before reaching Lake City, angle **left** *(west) on C 2400 N toward the water tower and drive to Main Street (C 500 E). Turn* **left** *(south) and drive a short distance to C 2390 N (Liberty Street); turn* **right** *on Liberty and proceed west two miles to the Marker.*

13 Moultrie-Macon: The Marker is on the north side of the road (GPS: W 39°45'16.3", W 88°46'6.1").

MACON (DECATUR)

Macon County was incorporated in 1828, two years before Lincoln's arrival in Illinois. It was part of the Circuit from its formation in 1839 until 1854. They moved there in 1830, following a cousin of Lincoln's mother named John Hanks, who had migrated there two years earlier. John's brother, William, had come earlier than that, settling on 80 acres immediately south of what would be Decatur's Lincoln Square. John's glowing reports drew Thomas Lincoln, who moved his family, including Abraham, to the north bank of the Sangamon, several miles southwest of Decatur. The Lincolns' first year in Illinois was difficult—malaria in the summer, followed by the infamous "Winter of the Deep Snow." Abraham Lincoln left Macon County in a canoe on the Sangamon in the spring of 1831, only to return repeatedly as a lawyer on the Eighth Judicial Circuit and for several major political events before he passed through on his way to Washington in 1861. His family left later in the spring of 1831, moving south and east to rural Coles County.

> *Proceed west into Macon County driving from the Marker to a T intersection, Farrell Road (Macon 60). Turn **right** and drive 0.6 miles to Sefton Road. Turn **left** on Sefton and proceed across 85th Street to the intersection with IL 121. Turn **right** and go around a curve on IL 21, then proceed into Mt. Zion and prepare to take a **left** turn on Elwin Road. Follow Elwin west through Mt. Zion. Continue west to a stop sign at Baltimore Road. Proceed 1.5 miles west to Turpin Road. Turn **right** (north) and follow a series of curves—although it seems like the same road, the name actually changes. It curves **left** and becomes Highland Road, then it curves **right** and becomes Turpin Road again. It then turns **left** and becomes South Shore Drive. Follow South Shore Drive to a stoplight at First Drive. After the stoplight, take the immediate first **right** (dead end) and proceed to Lake Decatur and the historical marker.*

 Lincoln Crossing

This is the location of the ferry across the Sangamon, which began operating in 1829, and the Lincolns probably used it. The Lincoln family headed north along what is now S. Main Street into the tiny hamlet of Decatur.

> *Return to a stop sign, make a **right**, and proceed across the dam. Because Main Street is a one-way street heading south, you will have to take Franklin to go north into downtown. As you pass the post office prepare to turn **left** (west) on Williams Street. Turn **left** (west) on Williams and proceed to N. Main Street. Turn **left** (south) on N. Main and continue to the intersection of N. Main and E. Main and park.*

CITY OF DECATUR

The city was platted in 1829 with a mandate to be laid out like Shelbyville, consisting of four large blocks around a public square. The south edge of the city was Wood Street, east was Water Street, north was Prairie Street, and west was Church Street. The four large blocks were divided by an east-west Main Street and a north-south Main Street, which intersect in the square now known as Lincoln Square. The fact that this area has two Main Streets demands particular attention when following directions, since there is an E. Main and a W. Main as well as a N. Main and a S. Main.

When the Lincolns' two-wagon caravan arrived on March 14, 1830, the village consisted of a handful of cabins, a log courthouse still under construction, and a store. Lincoln was a rough, uneducated, 21-year-old farm hand in homemade clothes. When he passed through Decatur on a train 31 years later, he was a leading Illinois lawyer, dressed in a Brooks Brothers suit, on his way to assume the presidency of the United States. Decatur was 40 times bigger than when he first arrived, and the junction of two great railroads. The parallel courses of Lincoln and Central Illinois speak volumes about the impact the man had on the place, and the place on the man.

Walking Tour of Lincoln Square and Downtown Lincoln Sites

There are several wayside exhibits mentioned in the walking tour that you are urged to read, but they are not included as numbered wayside exhibits in this guidebook, because they do not relate to Lincoln's law practice.

Decatur's Lincoln Square witnessed more important events during Lincoln's years in Illinois than any other area. He and his family arrived here at the end of their migration from Indiana, and it was the site of his first political speech, two courthouses in which he practiced law, the hotel (Cassell House) where his antislavery strategy of 1856 was launched, and the last speech of the Douglas Campaign. Although only legal sites are noted in this book, you should explore further for more of the story here.

Proceed to the southeast corner of the intersection of N. Main and E. Main and walk south one-half block to the Wayside Exhibit.

Wayside Exhibit 45: "Coming to Illinois"

The Lincolns spent their first night in Decatur here, sleeping on the ground. The second courthouse, constructed in 1838, stood on this now-vacant land. When he passed through Decatur from Danville to Bloomington in May 1856, Lincoln strolled through this area, showing his companions where he and his family had spent their first night. The exhibit also describes the original platting of the town.

Walk north across E. Main to the northeast corner.

🏃 Wayside Exhibit 46: This exhibit tells the story of Lincoln's first speech. It is also depicted here in a statue by sculptor Anthony Vestuto. It is probable that Lincoln was working on the farm of William Hanks, whose cabin was located at what is 452 W. Main Street today. Logs from the cabin are reputed to be part of the structure of this existing late nineteenth-century home.

Return south across E. Main and walk west across S. Main to the southwest corner.

🎩 This miniature replica of the first Macon County Courthouse marks the location of that log building, which may not have been completed by the time the Lincolns arrived. John Hanks was paid $9.87½ cents for "chinking and daubing" on the original building, which served as the county courthouse until it was replaced in 1838. Lincoln handled a few cases in it before it was replaced.

Return to the southeast corner of the intersection and the Wayside Exhibit that faces north.

Decatur's first courthouse, originally moved to Fairview Park, is now located at the Macon County History Museum. The identity of the people in this picture is unknown.

🏃 Wayside Exhibit 47: "Lincoln on the Circuit"

The Lincoln-era courthouse (1838–91), the county's second, formerly stood here. The exhibit features a period painting of the square looking to the east and a general description of Lincoln's practice in Decatur. From 1831 until 1839, during Lincoln's early practice in Decatur, Macon County was in the First Judicial Circuit. It joined the Eighth in 1839.

Walk south on Main to E. Wood Street, then east to S. Water Street and cross Wood to the Macon County building that houses the Macon County courts. Stop in front of the statue.

🎩 This statue by Morris Lovet-Lorski, titled *Lincoln the Lawyer*, was placed here in 1946. There is no Courthouse Marker here, or at any other courthouse site. Directions provided in this chapter will take you to the last Marker, which is located west of downtown.

Recross Wood to the northeast corner of Wood and Water.

🎩 As you follow the directions to the next Circuit site, you will pass five Wayside Exhibits, four of which tell the story of the Republican State Convention in May 1860, where delegates were selected for the National Convention in Chicago the following week. Significantly, the delegation was directed by the vote of the convention to unanimously support Lincoln. Bas reliefs by sculptor John McClarey accompany several of these exhibits.

Walk one-half block north on the east side of Water to the Wayside Exhibit.

🏃 Wayside Exhibit 48: "The Biggest Man"

The portrait of Lincoln chosen for the cover of this book was taken on May 9, 1860, by Edward Barnwell of Decatur. He requested the opportunity to photograph the "biggest man at the convention." The next day Lincoln received the unanimous endorsement for president. Lost for many years, the picture was presented to the Decatur Public Library by Barnwell's daughter, Grace, in 1947.

Continue north on Water to N. Park Street. Walk east on North Park, across Franklin Avenue, and then north to the corner of Franklin and Prairie.

Lincoln often stayed at the Revere House.

The hotel, then known as the Macon House, started in 1839 with 12 rooms on two floors. As Decatur grew, the hotel was expanded to the size shown here and became known as the Revere House. It was Decatur's most hospitable hotel and an island of comfort for the traveling lawyers.

Wayside Exhibit 49: "Music Please Maestro"

Jane Johns, wife of wealthy Decatur resident H. C. Johns, purchased a piano for their palatial home, which was under construction. When the piano arrived at the hotel where they were staying, it was too heavy to lift down from the wagon and then up into the hotel. Lincoln, who was also staying at the hotel, suggested that planks could run from the wagon to the hotel entrance so the piano could be wheeled without having to be lifted. In return for this kindness, Mrs. Johns accompanied the singing Circuit lawyers on the piano late into the evening.

Recross Franklin to Central Park. Walk back through the south side of the park. Continue south on Water, cross E. Main, and then walk west to return to Lincoln Square.
Return to your car to drive to the next site.

This ends your walking tour.

The next series of Lincoln sites in Decatur will be divided *east* and *west* of Lincoln Square.

EAST. *Proceed south on S. Main to Wood. Turn* **left** *(east) on Wood and proceed across Martin Luther King Jr. Drive to S. Hilton Street. Turn* **left** *(north) and proceed on Hilton to an unmarked T intersection. Turn* **left** *(west) onto the street adjacent to the tracks, then proceed to the* **right** *(north), parallel to the tracks, to a* **right** *turn (east), which is North Street. Stop. This is the site of Union Station.*

 The station included a decent hotel known as the Central House, or the Junction House, where Lincoln occasionally stayed, as he did during the 1860 Convention. His final appearance in Decatur occurred on February 11 as he journeyed to Washington, D.C. He made a brief address at the back of the train before walking through the crowd, shaking hands and greeting people. After a few moments, he got back on the train and continued east, leaving Decatur for the last time.

The Union Station, built in 1856 by the Illinois Central Railroad, sat at the southeast corner of the junction of the Great Western tracks running east-west and the Illinois Central tracks running north-south. Lincoln used this station to switch railroads as he traveled the Circuit for law and politics.

*Proceed east to Calhoun Street, then turn **left** (north) to Eldorado Road. Turn **right** (east) on Eldorado and follow US Route 36 southeasterly for 3.3 miles to its intersection with Airport Road at the southwest corner of the airport (follow the "Airport" sign). Turn **left** (north) and take Airport Road past the airport to North Fork Road. Turn **right** (east) and proceed to the Macon County History Museum.*

 Wayside Exhibit 50: "Macon County History Museum"

 The Macon County History Museum displays the story of Lincoln in Macon County. "Pioneer Village," which is behind the museum, is a collection of vintage buildings, one of which is the first Macon County Courthouse.

WEST. *Return to US 36 on Airport Road and turn **right** (west), and following US 36 west to Eldorado. Go **left** (south) on Eldorado, preparing to turn **left** on US 51, N. Main Street. Turn **left** on N. Main and proceed south to W. Main. Turn **right** (west) and proceed to 820 W. Main.*

 Wayside Exhibit 51: "Getting There from Here"
This exhibit in front of the stately Millikin House tells of Lincoln's Circuit travels. It includes a map of the Eighth Judicial Circuit and describes Main Street as a major route in and out of Decatur at the time. It tells how, during his Circuit travels, Lincoln rescued a pig from a "muddy pit," an encounter that did little to add to his lawyerly appearance.

The county's Courthouse Marker is placed at the Millikin Home instead of its customary location at the county courthouse.

Proceed west on Main Street to the campus of Millikin University.

This Lincoln statue by Fred M. Torrey, on the north side of Main, is titled *At Twenty-One I Came to Illinois.*

*Turn around and proceed east on W. Main and return to Lincoln Square. Turn **right** (south) on N. Main (US 51).*

This 1883 painting looks south on Lincoln Square and includes the second courthouse with its cupula and the Cassell House. This is the route that Lincoln probably would have taken as he left town to continue his journey around the Circuit.

 This is the route shown on the 1883 painting of the square. You are heading out of town as Lincoln would have.

The 1840 County Bridge replaced the ferry that had operated here when Lincoln entered Decatur in 1830. He used the bridge as he rode the Circuit in and out of Decatur.

*Drive south across the river, preparing to turn **right** on IL 105. Turn **right** (west) on IL 105 and proceed to IL 48. Turn **left** (south) on IL 48 and proceed 2.8 miles to Mount Auburn Road (C 3100 E, Macon County 28). Note your mileage at this intersection to determine the location of the tavern known as the Thirty-Three Mile House 2.2 miles to the west. Turn **right** (west) and proceed toward Mount Auburn.*

The Mount Auburn Road is part of the historic road from Terre Haute to Springfield, which also went through Mount Auburn on its way to Taylorville. The road runs parallel to the Sangamon River as it flows west. Proceed west as the traveling lawyers would have.

Drive 2.2 miles to a T intersection with Peru Road and stop.

William Warnick was Macon County's first sheriff and tax collector, a man of considerable influence in the young county. His log cabin, 100 yards west of this intersection on the north side of the road, stood on his

The Thirty-Three Mile House was built just west of this intersection around the log-cabin home of William Warnick in 1833. Lincoln stayed here on occasion.

farm, and was about 2.5 miles southeast of the Lincoln homestead on the north side of the Sangamon. Throughout his adult life, Lincoln cultivated influential people that he met. Warnick was one of the earliest. Lincoln had worked as a farmhand for him when he was younger. One winter, Lincoln fell through the ice crossing the Sangamon River on his way to Warnick's. He stayed with the family for several days, and Mrs. Warnick tended to his frozen feet. The Warnicks had a daughter named Mary, and it may have been on her account that the treatment took so long. Lincoln established a strong relationship with William Warnick and later did legal work for him. In 1843 John Eckel acquired the house and converted it to the Thirty-Three Mile House, named after the distance from Springfield. The plans to restore the building ended when a fire destroyed it in 1975.

Proceed west on Mount Auburn Road through several series of curves and continue west to the next County Line Marker at the intersection with C 4400 S (Meridian).

14 Macon-Christian: This Marker is on the south side of the road (GPS: N 39°46'59.8", W 89°09'19.3").

CHRISTIAN (TAYLORVILLE)

Christian County was formed in 1839 as part of the legislation that also created Menard and Logan Counties. It was formed from portions of Sangamon to the north, Shelby to the east, and Montgomery to the west. The county was initially named Dane County in honor of Nathan Dane of Massachusetts, who introduced the amendment to the Northwest Ordinance of 1787 that banned slavery north of the Ohio River. This offended the area's residents, mostly from Kentucky, who petitioned to change it. Their legislator, Abraham Lincoln, accomplished this, and Christian became the only county in Illinois whose name was changed. The residents were heavily Democratic, and voted against Lincoln in 1858, 1860, and 1864. Christian was a part of the Circuit from the county's formation until it was removed by Lincoln's bill in 1853. The Circuit court session in Christian was the last of each term, so Taylorville was known as the "Last Stop."

Mount Auburn provides views such as this.

TOWN OF MOUNT AUBURN

*Proceed west on Mount Auburn Road from the Marker. Look west to see Mount Auburn, a glacial kame rising 75 feet above the prairie. Proceed to C 1500 E, turn **left** and take the first **right** (C 2900 N) up the mount to the square. Stop at the T intersection.*

Mount Auburn was the first town in the area that became Christian County. A sign on the east side of the town square marks the site of the Nichols Hotel where Lincoln stayed in 1834, probably on his way to Vandalia for the December legislative session. It was likely a Circuit stop as well, about halfway between Decatur and Taylorville. In 1840, Lincoln succeeded in passing a bill authorizing the survey and platting of Mount Auburn.

*Turn **right** and proceed around the square to S. Broad Street. Turn **right** (south) on S. Broad and proceed to an unmarked T intersection (Arch Street). Turn **right** (west) on Arch and proceed to a T intersection, C 1400 E. Turn **left** and proceed south approximately 15 miles into Taylorville. Turn **right** on Bidwell Street, and then make an immediate **left** at the road's intersection with IL 29, which continues south as Webster Street toward downtown. Turn **left** on Webster.*

CITY OF TAYLORVILLE

The three commissioners selecting the county seat surprisingly chose the unsettled area that is now Taylorville because it was the center of the new county. The selection disappointed the two towns flanking the site, Allenton to the northeast (now gone) and Edinburg on the northwest, now swallowed up by Taylorville. (The original Edinburg is not to be confused with the existing town northwest of Taylorville.) The town was named for Springfield's real estate speculator, John Taylor, who was a friend of Lincoln's and one of the commissioners who selected the site.

*Upon entering Taylorville on Webster, proceed south to Market Street, turn **left** (east), drive to the courthouse square, and park your car.*

Walking Tour of the Square in Taylorville

The first courthouse served from 1840 to 1856 and now stands on the grounds of the Christian County Historical Society (see directions following the walking tour). The second courthouse was built in 1856. The long-time Circuit clerk Horatio M. Vandeveer engaged Lincoln to represent the county in contract litigation arising out of its construction—a case Lincoln lost in the Illinois Supreme Court.

Enter the courthouse at the south entrance.

This photograph shows the county's first two courthouses. The second courthouse sits in the center of the square. The first, a frame building with a peaked roof, was moved to the east side of the square, where it can be seen in this picture on the right.

An exhibit titled "Footprints of Lincoln in Christian County" is located in the east corridor on the first floor. It tells the story of Lincoln the legislator pushing the bill that created Christian County through the assembly in 1839. It describes complex title litigation involving Lincoln. The exhibit also includes records of Christian County Civil War soldiers lost in the Vicksburg campaign.

Emerge from the courthouse and walk to the northeast corner of the square.

 The Courthouse Marker is located here.

 The home of Horatio M. Vandeveer, the first house in Taylorville, was constructed in the middle of the block on the north side of the street.

Proceed to the middle of the block on the north side of the courthouse.

Wayside Exhibit 52: "Lincoln's Taylorville"
The Marker tells that Lincoln represented a man from Taylorville named Samuel Brown who chased trespassers from his watermelon patch by

The lawyers stayed at the Long House, operated by the family of Civil War casualty Francis Long. The hotel stood across the street on the opposite northeast corner. David Davis wrote home in 1850: "I had good accommodations at Taylorville with Mr. Lincoln and Mr. Thornton."

discharging his shotgun. Lincoln obtained the dismissal of the case, but, after the case was dismissed, Lincoln had to sue Brown for his fee of $6.20.

 Lincoln's client, Brown, recalled Lincoln sitting on the woodpile on the north side of the courthouse and telling stories late into the evening during court sessions.

Continue to the northwest corner of the square.

Wayside Exhibit 53: "The First County Courthouse"

 This exhibit discusses Lincoln's law practice in Christian County and includes the story depicted by the John McClarey statue of Lincoln and a pig, which stands near the exhibit. Lincoln was interrupted during a closing argument by hogs rooting under the raised first courthouse. Lincoln asked Judge Davis for a "Writ of Quietus" ordering the sheriff to remove the noisy swine.

Walk south to Market, cross Washington Street and Market, and walk west to the next Wayside Exhibit.

Wayside Exhibit 54: "Friend Vandeveer"
This exhibit tells the story of Lincoln and his close friend, Horatio M. Vandeveer.

Horatio M. Vandeveer began his career in Springfield before moving to Taylorville. He raised a company that fought in the Mexican War. Over his lifetime, he eventually held nine different offices. He had more cases in association with and against Lincoln than any other lawyer in the county. Lincoln also represented him on several cases. His friendship with Lincoln demonstrates Lincoln's ability to separate his law practice from his politics.

Vandeveer was an attorney, a Democrat, and the most influential politician in Christian County.

This two-story stagecoach stop was built here by Robert Allen. Lincoln stayed here as he traveled to and from Vandalia. The land had been mortgaged to his friend, Joshua Speed, for $900. When Allen defaulted, Speed foreclosed with the help of Lincoln, his lawyer.

One of the cases Lincoln and Vandeveer tried together was against attorney Silas Robbins of Springfield. During the proceedings, Robbins responded to a point that Lincoln had made: "If that is true, I will agree to eat this desk." Lincoln quickly replied, "If you do eat that desk, I hope it will come out a brand new manufactured wagon."

This ends your walking tour.

Drive east from the north side of the courthouse on Main Cross Street across Park Street (IL 29) to the first **left**, *the Christian County Historical Museum. Turn* **left** *immediately before reaching IL 48.*

The most important building at the museum grounds is the first courthouse, in which Lincoln regularly appeared. It was moved here from the square. Be sure to observe the other interesting buildings and exhibits at this museum.

Note your mileage when you leave the museum and proceed back west on Main Cross to its intersection with Park (IL 29). Turn **right** *(north) on IL 29* *and proceed west then north toward Edinburg. After driving 9.1 miles from the museum, turn **left** (west) on the county road at the sign for Edinburg. Proceed west, then north into Edinburg. Turn **left** to a Wayside Exhibit at the northeast corner of Grant and Washington Streets.*

🏃 Wayside Exhibit 55: "The Great Eastern Stagecoach"

This is not the Edinburg of Lincoln's day, which preceded Taylorville. A man named Robert Allen acquired 160 acres in what was then known as Blue Point, which became the new Edinburg in 1863. Allen obtained the rights to carry the mail from Springfield to Terre Haute.

*Return to IL 29 and proceed north to C 2300 N. Turn **left** to an immediate T intersection, C 2300 N. Turn **right** on C 2300 N and proceed around a curve to the west, then to a small bridge across a brook.*

15 Christian-Sangamon: The Marker is on the north side of the road, on the west bank of a babbling brook (GPS N 39°40'7", W 89°12'51.7").

This County Line Marker sits on an east-west road but in fact marks the north-south road, which once ran parallel to IL 29. Lincoln would have taken the north-south road on his way home to Springfield. You'll also see two county road signs indicating that this was once an intersection.

*Return to IL 29 and proceed into Springfield. Upon entering the city, proceed west to 9th Street, turn **right** (north), and return to Lincoln's home.*

Like Lincoln, you have returned home after the trip around the Circuit.

Once a lawyer was going on endlessly while arguing his case before an exasperated and bored Judge David Davis. Davis finally interrupted him and requested that Lincoln, who was standing in the back of the courtroom, approach the bench. He asked Lincoln to tell the loquacious man the story of the long-winded preacher. Lincoln responded to Davis by telling of a parishioner who finally summoned up the courage to inquire of his church's preacher why his sermons were so long. The preacher responded, "Oh, I know my sermons are too long, but once I get going, I am just too lazy to quit."
Taking Lincoln's advice, I quit.

The welcome scene that Lincoln would have viewed as he returned from the long ride around the Eighth Judicial Circuit is depicted here in an early winter November snowstorm.

APPENDIX
FOR FURTHER READING
ILLUSTRATION CREDITS
INDEX

APPENDIX

Counties and County Seats of the Eighth Judicial Circuit, 1839–61

County	County Seat	1839–41	1841–42	1843–45	1845–47	1847–53	1853–57	1857–61
Christian (originally Dane County)	Taylorville							
DeWitt	Clinton							
Livingston	Pontiac							
Logan	Postville (1839–47) Mt. Pulaski (1847–54) Lincoln (1854–present)							
Macon	Decatur							
McLean	Bloomington							
Menard	Petersburg							
Sangamon	Springfield							
Tazewell	Tremont (1839–51) Pekin (1851–present)							
Champaign	Urbana							
Mason	Havana							
Moultrie	Sullivan							
Piatt	Monticello							
Shelby	Shelbyville							
Woodford	Versailles (1841–43) Metamora (1843–96) Eureka (1896–present)							
Edgar	Paris							
Vermilion	Danville							

Note: Shaded cells indicate years in which counties were part of the Eighth Judicial Circuit.

Source: Compiled from Martha L. Banner, Cullom Davis, eds., *The Law Practice of Abraham Lincoln, Complete Documentary Edition*, DVD (Champaign: University of Illinois Press, 2000); Jesse White, *Origins and Evolution of Illinois Counties* (Springfield: Secretary of State, State of Illinois, 2006). Originally appeared in Guy C. Fraker, *Lincoln's Ladder to the Presidency: The Eighth Judicial Circuit* (Carbondale: Southern Illinois University Press, 2012).

FOR FURTHER READING

Andreasen, Bryon C. *Looking for Lincoln in Illinois: Lincoln and Mormon Country*. Carbondale: Southern Illinois University Press, 2015.

———. *Looking for Lincoln in Illinois: Lincoln's Springfield*. Carbondale: Southern Illinois University Press, 2015.

Fraker, Guy C. *Lincoln's Ladder to the Presidency: The Eighth Judicial Circuit*. Carbondale: Southern Illinois University Press, 2012.

———. "The Real Lincoln Highway: The Forgotten Lincoln Circuit Markers." *Journal of the Abraham Lincoln Association* 25, no. 1 (2004): 76–97.

Krause, Susan. *From Log Cabins to Temples of Justice: Courthouses in Lincoln's Illinois—a Publication of the Lincoln Legal Papers*. Papers of Abraham Lincoln. Springfield: Illinois Historic Preservation Agency, 2000.

Shaw, Robert, and Michael Burlingame. *Abraham Lincoln Traveled This Way: The America Lincoln Knew*. Heyworth, IL: Firelight Publishing, in association with John Warner IV, 2013.

Wilson, Douglas L. *Honor's Voice: The Transformation of Abraham Lincoln*. New York: Knopf, 1998.

ILLUSTRATION CREDITS

All maps were created by Tom Willcockson of Mapcraft Cartography specifically for this book. Images were prepared for publication by Ann Charback of JMC, and the presentation of the maps and the icons was prepared by Bill Edwards of the Copy Shop, both in Bloomington, Illinois. All images in this book are courtesy of the Abraham Lincoln Presidential Library and Museum, except for the following:

Individuals

- George Buss, Freeport, Illinois—Leonard Swett, p. 36.
- Melissa Chambers, Champaign, Illinois—Benjamin F. Harris Home, p. 58; Benjamin F. Harris, p. 59.
- Guy C. Fraker, Bloomington, Illinois—County Line Marker, p. 5; Courthouse Marker, p. 6; Wayside Exhibit, p. 6; *Daily Illinois State Journal* advertisements, p. 12; Panther Creek Ford, p. 25; Logan County Courthouse, Mt. Pulaski, p. 43; *Young Lawyer*, by Lorado Taft, p. 63.
- Chuck Hand, Paris, Illinois—Portrait of Kirby Benedict, p. 81.
- Rachel Reed and Sarah Bitzer, Shelbyville, Illinois—Home of Anthony Thornton, p. 94.
- Janet Roney, Sullivan, Illinois—First Moultrie County Courthouse, p. 96.
- Mark S. Walsh, Delavan, Illinois—Delavan House, Phillips House, p. 16; Registration at Delavan House, p. 17.
- Chuck Watson, Springfield, Illinois—Letcher Basin Panorama, p. 26; Mount Auburn view, p. 108.

Institutional Repositories

- Allerton Public Library, Monticello, Illinois—Tenbrook Hotel, p. 57.
- Champaign County Historical Archives, Urbana Free Library, Urbana, Illinois—Joseph Cunningham, p. 63; Samuel Alschuler image of Lincoln, p. 64; American House Hotel, p. 64;

Registry of the American House, p. 65; 1848 Champaign County Courthouse, Urbana, p. 66; Kelley's Tavern, p. 67.
- Decatur Public Library Local History Collection, Decatur, Illinois—First Macon County Courthouse, p. 100; Revere House, p. 102; Union Station, p. 103; Lincoln Square Looking South, p.105; 1840 County Bridge, p. 105; Thirty-Three Mile House, p. 106.
- Edgar County Historical Society, Paris, Illinois—Edgar County Courthouse, p. 81; Courthouse Square, p. 82; Court Street Looking East, p. 83.
- McLean County Museum of History, Bloomington, Illinois—Jesse Fell Home, p. 30; Jesse Fell, p. 30; Sarah Davis and daughter, Sally, p. 31; Asahel Gridley, p. 32; McLean County Courthouse, p. 33; Phoenix Block, p. 36; Pike House, p. 37.
- Shelby County Historical and Genealogical Society, Shelbyville, Illinois—Black Horse Tavern, p. 90; Shelbyville Courthouse Square, p. 91; Lincoln-Thornton Debate, Robert Root Painting, p. 92; Main Street Shelbyville, p. 93.
- Tazewell County Genealogical and Historical Society, Pekin, Illinois—Tazewell County Courthouse, p. 18; Tazewell House, p. 21.
- United States District Court, Central District of Illinois, Sue E. Myerscough, U.S. District Judge—Samuel H. Treat, p. 3.
- University of Illinois, Urbana, Illinois, *Lincoln: Prelude to the Presidency*, WILL TV, Urbana, Illinois © Board of Trustees, 2009—Interior, Mt. Pulaski Courthouse, p. 47.
- US Bank NA, Taylorville, Illinois—Long House, p. 110.
- Vermilion County Museum Society, Danville, Illinois—McCormack House, p. 72; Lincoln Hall, p. 72; photograph of Lincoln, by Amon T. Joslin, p. 73; Panorama of Danville Courthouse Square, p. 73; Barnum Building, p. 74; Ward Hill Lamon, p. 74; Danville Newspaper Ad, p. 75; Oscar Harmon, p. 75; Elizabeth Harmon, p. 75; Oliver Davis, p. 76; Danville Depot, p. 76; Enoch Kingsbury, p. 77; William Fithian, p. 78.
- Vespasian Warner Public Library District Special Collections, Clinton, Illinois—DeWitt County Courthouse, p. 50.

Publications

- Robert Shaw, photography, and Michael Burlingame, narrative, *Abraham Lincoln Traveled This Way: The America Lincoln Knew* (Heyworth, IL.: Firelight Publishing, in association with John Warner IV, 2013)—Thunderstorm over the Lincoln Trail Road, p. 68; Witness Oaks, Vermilion County, Illinois, p. 69; Snowfall at the Eighth Street Home of Abraham and Mary Lincoln, Springfield, Illinois, p. 114.

Public Domain Publications

- Bernhardt Wall, *Following Abraham Lincoln, 1809–1865* (New York: Wise, Parslow Company, 1943)—Green Tree Hotel, p. 83; Edinburg Stagecoach Stop, p. 112.

INDEX

GUY C. FRAKER, a retired attorney from Bloomington, Illinois, is the author of *Lincoln's Ladder to the Presidency: The Eighth Judicial Circuit*. He consulted on the documentary *Lincoln: Prelude to the Presidency* and cocurated *Prologue to the Presidency: Abraham Lincoln on the Illinois Eighth Judicial Circuit*, an exhibit on permanent display at the David Davis Mansion in Bloomington. A graduate of the University of Illinois College of Law, he is a former president of the McLean County Bar Association.

LOOKING FOR LINCOLN HERITAGE COALITION

BOARD OF DIRECTORS
Guy Fraker, Chair
Robert Davis
Lauren Groff
Gerry Kettler
Laura Marks
Matthew Mittelstaedt
Daniel Noll
Dale Phillips
John Potocki

STAFF
Sarah Watson, Executive Director
Jeanette Cowden
Heather Wickens

BOOK COMMITTEE
Dr. Bryon Andreasen
Dana Homann
Matthew Mittelstaedt
Kim Rosendahl
Sylvia Frank Rodrigue
Tim Townsend
Dr. Samuel Wheeler
Sarah Watson
Heather Wickens